AF444808

FOREWORD

Most of my life I did not know why I cared so much for the opinions of others and why I needed the validation of women so much, encouraging me to experience several abusive and stormy relationships. Thanks to María de León Crowhurst, I understood the reason better.

For many years I gave training to help people transform their lives. Note that there were few people who had wonderful growth and a large majority were constantly stuck. I thought to only solution was to strive to live better.

I understood that in many cases, although the person put his effort to change what did not favor him, his life did not flourish anyway. I even had the possibility of finding in me, behaviors that returned like ruthless ghosts, from time to time, to re-sabotage my life and mutilate my dreams. My intuition told me that there was something else I could not see yet. The answer was beyond my birth.

My first brother, Hugo, died at birth. Situation that marked the life of my parents. My mother, when she learned that she was pregnant with my second brother, Axel, clung to all the care so that her baby was born well. She, my mother, had always wanted to have a daughter, but at that moment, what mattered most was that her baby was born alive. So it was, and my brother initiated his journey in this lifetime.

A couple of years later, it was me, who came into the world; but they didn't wait for me. While waiting for me, my mother lived through her pregnancy with the dream that I was a girl. At that time there was no way to know the sex of the baby, so my mom just held on to her desire. All that illusion fell apart when she was told that I was another baby boy.

Not that my mom didn't love me, she did; but I did not meet her expectations ... ever! The disagreement was so great that it marked my life. Much of my existence I had experienced the belief of "I am almost there, I will make it, but not yet." And when adolescence arrived, every woman was the opportunity to show my mother's archetype that I was worthy of being loved.

María de León Crowhurst, through this wonderful book, will show you how important it is your mother's pregnancy and your birth on your present sentimental life. She has hundreds of documented cases and decades of years of experience revealing each of the mysteries that the pregnancy holds. In a completely clear way and through the history of several of its cases, it will give you the opportunity to discover your own history; The hidden truth of your suffering in love.

Your relationship will never be the same after reading this book. And even better, the relationship with yourself will become a cascade of acceptance, understanding and love for yourself; that this time, it won't end.

If you are willing to discover yourself, to enlighten yourself, then continue reading.

Ariel Ortuño
contacto@arielortuno.com
BestSeller Author and Speaker
You are a phrase of inspiring the world ...

INTRODUCTION

Did your prenatal life was in a sanctuary?

Were you offered hell against your will?

What memories and beliefs are really yours?

Are you true to yourself? Who do you think you are?

This book will help you understand where certain emotions come from and why sometimes you feel anxiety, frustration, impatience, pain, confusion, hopelessness, depression, sadness, anger, apathy, the feeling of loneliness, of rejection, of abandonment, amongst many others that do not contribute to your wish of leading a full and happy life.

Here we will talk about the importance of gestating a baby in optimal physical, mental and spiritual health conditions.

Many times, you have heard someone asking a pregnant woman: and when do you get better? As if pregnancy were a disease or something that was wrong.

Little by little the understanding of this beautiful experience has changed and today we hear people asking a pregnant woman: and when do you give birth? or when is your baby born?

Pregnancy can be a perfect state in women, as long as she is mentally, emotionally and physically prepared for it. When this happens, they are months of joy, yearnings, dreams and illusion. Getting pregnant, without awareness of the responsibility so great that it is to bring a human being into the world, is to demonstrate lack of love for what is creation and emotional immaturity.

The baby since she is pregnant is the most vulnerable being on Earth. He has no power of decision, he moves and expresses himself within the womb, sometimes these movements pass imperceptibly to the mother and in others they are quite noticeable; depending on the emotions of the mother, her health, her tranquility, her joy, sadness, pain, emotion, discouragement, disappointment, etc.

The unborn baby's vulnerability depends mainly on the mother. The father, present or not, contributes directly and indirectly to the emotions that the mother has, the ideal is to be the person responsible for protecting her.

What happens when there is not a father's figure. The most common situation is that the unborn baby begins its life with a certain disability. Let's be fair in this. A dad may not be present for several reasons: he got the woman pregnant and left, he is the biological father, but he doesn't get involved in the pregnancy process; he is sick; he could be traveling; works too much and is not at home, he does not participate in the period of the pregnancy; has died; the couple is in the process of divorce; they have serious conflicts between them and ignores or mistreats his wife, etc. etc.

There are situations above the baby's control that can upset their intrauterine life, therefore, we need to study each case as unique.

It is urgent to raise awareness of what it is to bring a human being to this Planet Earth. Living here is an experience, so why not start that experience as something unique, unrepeatable and wonderful? We need a healthier society in all aspects. There is too much violence and hate between countries and amongst others.

I remember very much what the gynecologist said that attended me in my 2 pregnancies.

"The pregnant woman should be the first 3 months
of her pregnancy between cottons,
as in the last 3. "

Then what happens in those months precisely?

Well, the woman does not take notice of her pregnancy many times, until the 3rd. month! and at the end of pregnancy, if she has taken care of herself or has had a really good time or has complaint all the time feeling overwhelmed and working long hours, and being in the process of their pregnancy, they end up very stressed and tense at the end of the day.

Many women don't even stop working! They continue under these conditions for much of the pregnancy and wait until a week or days to give birth and suspend their work. I am talking about the countries in Latin America in which many women face the need to work to support a home or help the husband.

In some European countries, working pregnant women are licensed to stop working at 6th. month of pregnancy and must prepare their home for the arrival of the new family member, competent authorities support and supervise this whole arrangement, women look for who will help them and attend the first weeks, sometimes the government assigns them a person for that. In other countries the man is also licensed by the work to support his wife.

Because some women are stressed with responsibilities in their jobs, there are babies who come to this world exhausted, depressed, tired, upset and restless, unlike others who arrive in a state of joy, tranquility and peace since their mothers had the opportunity to live their pregnancy in the stillness and tranquility of his home environment.

There will be women who express that they 'need' to work for sustenance, then I ask myself, so why rush to a pregnancy?

Considering that bringing a child into the world is an act of responsibility in terms of protection, it is not wise to get pregnant when the economic, housing or tranquility situation in the home is not resolved. What happens then with these children who come to the world in conditions of poverty, scarcity, domestic violence, lack of love in a home?

They become a dysfunctional being unable to love, be loved or feel loved and the family is dysfunctional. It is not the best way to start life on this Planet.

CHAPTER 1: A LITTLE BIT OF MY STORY…

Since I was little, I remember that I had a great love for animals and children. Perhaps seeing that my brother, a year younger than me, had a cleft lip that did not allow him to speak well, then I began to help him; I stood in front of him and explained how he should speak correctly, and simply by the intuition that would lead me to become a teacher someday. I liked to play the teacher role with my friends and another thing that I loved were foreign languages; for me it was very important to be able to express myself and make myself understood with anyone. I only learned English and French apart from my native language, which is Spanish, a little Italian at the Conservatory of Music in Mexico City, since that language was required for the singing lessons.

English has been an excellent tool for me, since it has given me the opportunity to communicate with various people who have contributed to my intellectual growth and the ease of being able to read material to increase my knowledge. There are certain books about the subject I am interested in only written in that language. Helped me as well in order to be able to participate as a speaker in some Congresses and Seminars whose universal language is English.

A couple of years ago, in 2017, I stopped working as a teacher, although I remain active in music as a performer. Today I dedicate myself to counseling in a 100%, I am a life motivator, as I would call it, an activity that I had somehow been doing since 1990.

Having studied several Courses and Workshops at NLP and with my Certification as a Master in NLP, I think it is very important to motivate others to achieve their dreams and lead a more prosperous and happy life.

Very important is that women feel good when they become mothers and that children come to this world with a different quality of life. When talking about prosperity I am not referring exclusively to economic wealth; I am talking about helping people find their inner warrior spirit, the fighters they are, the spirit full of love for oneself and others that it is ultimately what will save this Planet. I read about associations that are dedicated to rescue animals, to rescue children, to rescue families, to rescue to rescue to rescue! And most of the time I ask myself, and who rescues the unborn baby? Not only a gynecologist cares in their periodic reviews, which end up being physical.

What about emotional care?

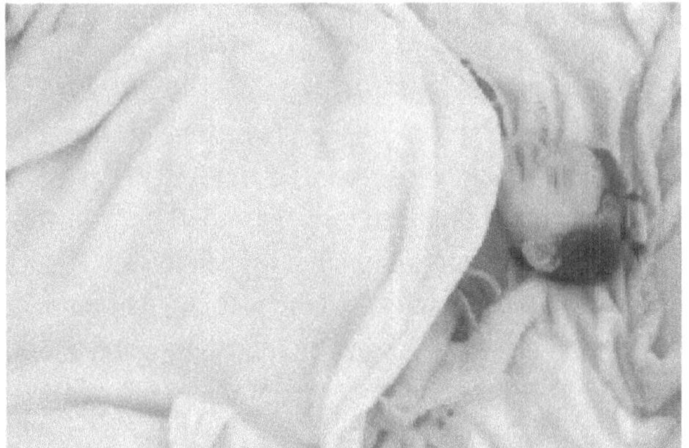

CHAPTER II: WHAT IS PRENATAL PSYCHOLOGY?

As the name says, the study of the psyche of unborn babies.

Dr. David B. Chamberlain (02/27/1928 - 05/01/2014), an American psychologist, was one of the founders and pioneers of the Association of Prenatal and Perinatal Psychology and Health (APPPAH). This Association is a charity, scientific organization for education, offers information, inspiration and support to professionals in medicine and health, parents who expect a child and all those interested in expanding their knowledge about the psychology around the pregnancy and childbirth in women.

They point out that it is essential to attend to the quality of life, of growth and of society itself. At the end of the day, they summarize it to:

"The ecology of the womb becomes the world ecology."

Chamberlain began using hypnotherapy in 1974 to discover and resolve the traumas that came from intrauterine life and at the time of the individual's birth. He showed that prenatal memories existed and that they were true and reliable. He served as president of APPPAH for 13 years. Author of several books including a bestseller " Babies Remember Birth ", in 1998 he changed the title to " The Mind of your Newborn Baby" as part of the X Celebration Anniversary of its publication; currently translated into 13 languages.

A book that I recommend reading to every woman who wants to become a mother, understand her children and understand herself. In 1996, he built the site www.birthpsychology.com together with Dr. Thomas Verny.

Dr. Chamberlain continued his research on the origins of prenatal memories and in 2013 he published "Windows of the Womb, Revealing the Conscious Baby from Conception to Birth."

Dr. Chamberlain talked about the uterus being like a classroom, unborn babies learn, remember, feel pain, and communicate. Due to their research in this regard and checking that unborn babies have a 'psyche' or soul from conception. He was characterized as a defense attorney of how changes should be made in the way newborns were treated. He wrote extensively about the crying of infants as a means of communication that is sometimes ignored when doing certain practices during his birth.

He was in favor of the midwives attending births to improve the treatment of babies at such crucial moments of their lives.

Dr. David Chamberlain died in May 2014, his legacy remains with us in his books and articles, as well as in the hearts of all who knew him. I had the pleasure of meeting him in a couple of congresses on Prenatal Psychology in September 1998 in London, England and February 2000 in San Francisco, California.

Another of the great founding doctors of APPPAH is Dr. Thomas Verny, a psychiatrist and disciple of Dr. Frederick Leboyer, author of a wonderful book entitled "Childbirth Without Violence" (published in 1975); same who wrote about the benefits of natural childbirth, without epidural. This was an advance in the procedures carried out at the time of delivery. Leboyer after 30 years of practice, leaves everything and began a radical psychoanalysis, yoga classes and went to India for 6 months, took music and singing lessons. After that he returns to Paris and at his birth clinic modifies his midwife techniques.

Dr. Leboyer, the first doctor who studied Birth Trauma. He talked a lot about respect for the baby when he came to this world. He talked about how to receive the baby, not as an object but as a human being. The importance was not in the woman who gives birth, but in the being born, since he is the one who strives to come into the world, the mother cooperates in this beautiful adventure. He was in favor of a gentle birth, with dim light, without pressure, that the baby was born in the most natural way possible, without the use of forceps; place the baby in the womb as soon as he leaves, give him a gentle massage so he can breathe: be born with respect. The fact that the mother holds the baby creates an indestructible maternal bond. He suggested not to cut the umbilical cord immediately, but to wait for the baby to breathe on his own.

Years later, Michel Odent and Thomas Verny collected hundreds of studies that had been carried out in the last 40 years about the perinatal period and find that the baby of course is a person who feels and remembers. All these investigations showed that what we suffer in adult life is a result of the trauma experienced and that it has developed in the womb and the moment of delivery.

Dr. Thomas Verny is the author of a wonderful book, "The Life of the Unborn Baby" another best seller. In the research conducted by Dr. Verny, he shows the importance of knowing that in the intrauterine life is the origin of the diseases of adult life. Unfortunately, this field is not being properly served by science.

Likewise, the physical, emotional and mental state of the parents before conceiving and after conception is very important. There are factors such as age, good nutrition, hormonal balance and lifestyle that affect the molecules that control the function of genes both in their children and in the generations to come.

It must be said that another of the great researchers and pioneers in Prenatal Psychology is Dr. William R. Emerson. It is among the most important figures in the world for being among the first to develop methods of prenatal and perinatal treatments for babies and children. He is the author of 5 books, 15 chapters published in Psychology journals among several other works. Dr. Emerson practiced Psychotherapy for 25 years, specializing in regressive therapy and lecturing on the subject in his country and internationally. It currently offers seminars and training in the United States, Canada and Europe.

Among the birth traumas he mentions are:

- The use of forceps. These are interventions that can symbolize, respectively, medical induction or mechanical induction of abortion attempts.
- Force the birth of the baby by pushing the mother's womb.

A practice that is still carried out even in some villages of my country by inexperienced people and this is a violent act for the unborn baby.

- Cesarean section. The shock caused by caesarean section is closely related to the sensation of a sudden, unexpected and fearful attack or change, all connected to the feeling of loss of control. The average time, from the moment of the incision until the baby is completely out, is less than a minute. It is a transition too fast for the baby, since they do not perceive anything before or are prepared for birth. They are not allowed to 'decide' when to be born.
- The use of anesthesia. Says Janov (1983), '... medication [anesthesia] crosses the placental barrier, sending several doses, hundreds of times, stronger than it can tolerate a baby, so that neither the baby nor the mother are able to react normally '. According to Shanley (1994), in 80% of hospital deliveries some analgesic and / or anesthesia is administered to the mother. Anesthesia causes trauma related to the emotional bond, shock syndromes, control complex, personality disorders, power complexes and abuse of certain substances.
- Attempt of abortion. It carries a feeling of rejection.
- Inductions with oxytocin. Shanley (1994), medications such as Pitocin and Oxytocin are used around 20-40% of all hospital births. They can produce effects such as affective bond deficiencies, shock, invasion / control complexes, productivity complexes, substance abuse and problems related to self-esteem.
- When the mother's cervix does not dilate.
- Baby in inadequate posture to exit through the vaginal canal.
- Umbilical cord around the neck. The feeling of suffocation is present.

'A study published in the British Medical Journal ensures that children born with forceps have a death rate of 34.9 per 1000.' Dr. Ata Pouramini in chiropractic care, woman, chiropractic for children, health, vertebral subluxations.

Unfortunately, pregnancy has become something taken as a disease. Women are increasingly disconnected from their bodies and babies, so they rely more on chemistry and surgical procedures. It is important to realize they have inner wisdom. It tells her which is, the best way to give birth. The horizontal position, in a birthing bed, is not the most recommended since there is no dynamism in the birth process, it should be walking, and squatting (thus the pelvis opens or be held by the arms of the husband or midwife) to help the baby to be born more easily, the law of gravity operates in this regard and a delivery can take place in less time. The woman must listen to her intuition, move as her body tells her.

Psychoanalyst Otto Rank mentions: 'All neurotic disorders have their origin in birth trauma. Birth originates a primitive anguish that is incorporated into the subject and is eliminated throughout life. '

Dr. David Chamberlain, author of Babies Remember Birth, (1988), says that while babies experience a variety of negative and positive experiences at birth, "it is rare for the baby to not experience any trauma".

Why is the incidence of birth trauma so high?

There are multiple reasons (Emerson, 1996), but the most logical seem to be the following:

- The industrialization of society and the growing importance and dependence of technology.
- The rise of "technological births".
- Increased stress in Western cultures (it is shown that prenatal stress increases the incidence of birth trauma)
- The increase in withdrawal syndrome in the fetus (both by alcoholism and drug addiction), unwanted pregnancies and prenatal abuse (more common in industrialized cultures than in agrarian).
- Maternal prenatal traumas resurface during childbirth and

affect how the experience of giving birth is perceived and lived.

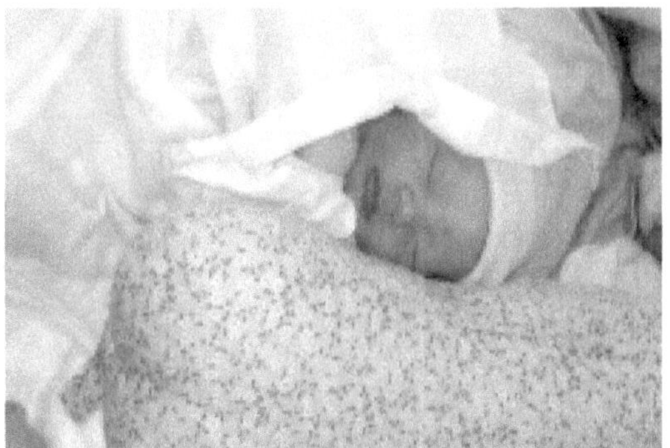

CHAPTER III: THE PSYCHOLOGY OF WHOLE-SELF

It is one of the most renowned therapies in the world. Created by Dr. Jon RG Turner and his wife Troya GN Turner.

Whole-self Therapy

Where the individual is helped to find the 4 cornerstones of his Emotional Intelligence. All this goes hand in hand with the investigations of Chamberlain and Verny.

Dr. Turner mentions that we are the result of emotions and feelings from 8 generations ago, so far proven. Can you imagine, how much to heal and rescue in individuals and in ourselves? We want a healthier society, we must turn our eyes to health during the prenatal life and prepare men and women to conceive and raise healthier and more stable human beings in all aspects, in a holistic way.

The stress in which one lives today does not contribute at all in a better and healthy society.

Environmental pollution, psychological, pesticides used in the fields, chemicals in the production of plastic containers, alcohol and nicotine, all this causes malformation in the brain of unborn children.

Jon RG Turner investigated in a non-hypnotic way the emotional patterns of the parents of his patients and were experimenting when they were expecting a baby. He discovers that we are not only a synthesis of the physical DNA of our parents, but we are also the synthesis of the burden of their emotions that they experienced during the 9 months that gestation lasted, what Turner calls the eDNA (emotional burden of DNA)

Every human being was born with a full menu of emotional patterns. Through the Psychology of Whole-Self, we were able to realize that the feelings of low self-esteem and patterns that have prevailed in our lives are really the residue of our parents' reactions to traumatic or important events within Pregnancies they had. for example: if the mother has been betrayed during her pregnancy, the child that will be born will bring with himself the belief of having been betrayed and lives a life without trusting others.

When the human being can recognize that the pattern of behavior, he has been living is nothing less than his mother's reaction to having been betrayed, he will be freed from this pattern of behavior. Whole-self is more than a common therapy, it offers an educational and philosophical basis for a Full-Life.

Dr. Jon RG Turner explains this in his fabulous therapeutic method. Co-creator of the same together with his wife Troy GN Turner-Groot.

The PAM (Prebirth Awakening Matrix) translated as: The Awakening of Prenatal Memories; It is the central jewel in the tiara that is composed of the Psychology, Philosophy and Education of the Whole-Self.

Let me quote what Dr. Jon RG Turner and Trojan GN Turner wrote:

> *'PAM leads me to past times to discover and awaken the source, the very root of the patterns that exist in my life to be in harmony. I allow myself , in a compassionate and safe way, to remember in a new conscious way, moments before my conception and moving on in time through an amazing journey that presents me with clear and deep images that lead me to understand, change and transform my lifetime.'*

The Psychology of Whole-Self is a gentle, loving, transpersonal and multidimensional educational process, through which we convert individual realities into objective truths.

Prenatal Memory Therapy was discovered by Dr. Jon RG Turner in his practice as a therapist in Beverly Hills, California. Dr. Turner is one of the pioneers in Prenatal Psychology. In the year of 1970, like David Chamberlain and William Emerson, he anticipates the concepts of neurolinguistics when they are not yet used as such. Whole-Self Discovery & Development , Inc. (WSDDI) is established in Santa Fe, New Mexico. Currently the Turners reside in Holland, they have taken the concept of Whole-Self to 30 countries. They have developed interesting innovations for 15 years, which leads us to see that they have been working in this specialty for almost half a century.

Dr. Turner writes:

REALITAS AD VERITATIS
I want to discover the truth of my reality
instead of living my reality as if it were the truth.
I turn my reality into the truth when I live with
alignment and harmony with my Whole-Self.
My Whole-Self is the totality of my own being,
He knows everything I've experienced.
My personality models my reality,
what I think has happened to me
and on a nonconscious level he continued to believe.
Objective truth is what actually happened,
and not what I think happened.
My Whole-Self wants me to recognize my reality,
making it my objective truth.

The Psychology of Whole-Self has evolved into a psychological, philosophical and educational process, through which the Source of Life of our Consciousness can be discovered and developed.

There is a phrase that is totally accurate within this method:

I CANNOT MODIFY SOMETHING IN MY LIFE,
UNTIL I DON'T KNOW PRECISELY
WHAT NEEDS TO BE MODIFIED!

Within the Psychology of Whole-Self we find four Laws of Life:

1. THE LAW OF OPPOSITION.
Everything that I oppose will have to experience it!
2. THE LAW OF CONFIRMATION
By opposing what I feel, I draw conclusions therefore, I confirm what happened.
3. THE LAW OF DECISION
Also called the Law of Creation. When I am opposing to

create and feel I judge myself sin a subconscious way, then
make decisions and / or make conclusions.
4. THE LAW OF REPETITION
Therefore, by doing all, of the above, this law is generated
that practically invites me to, try again!

Whole-self therapy leads us to explore in our past to understand what behaviors we can change and have a better quality of life.

It leads us to make a list of the most important situations or problems we have faced in life, whether we have resolved them or not. All kinds of problems that will be treated: emotional, physical, mental.

What I think it is a problem, what is happening, may be real, but it may not be the truth in the way I interpret it.

It is very important to know that everyone contributes to my resistance to change, since in them I see my behaviors reflected and of course I do not want to recognize them, therefore, I refuse to change them. It is also good to be aware that I cannot change others until I myself do not change, so they will change.

The people I've met throughout my life have served one purpose: my growth, my development and my evolution. Throughout my life, due to my life, the experiences I have had will leave me with a belief, so we are able to change our beliefs in an Objective Truth through this Whole-Self therapy.

One of the principles of Whole-Self says:

I HAVE NOT COME TO THIS LIFE TO CONTINUE REPEATING THE
SAME PATTERNS AND PESIMISTIC OR NEGATIVE SENSATIONS!
I HAVE COME TO WORK IN THEM, TO NEUTRALIZE THEM AND
CHANGE THEM TO OPTIMISTIC AND POSITIVE SENSATIONS.

It is interesting to find the triggers that can destroy our relationships. Whole-Self discovers them. Among the most important is the memory of the pain of trauma from being abandoned, that is a problem. The trigger is presented when we have a feeling of well-being and happiness. At that time the human being changes his behavior to avoid what his personality has created as 'what will happen to me when I feel happy?.......'They can leave me!

Then I end the relationship before they leave me. This is a limiting belief and thus the human being avoids the pain of being abandoned again. What you can notice there, is that the person damages himself.

One reality is, that in today's society there are more and more human beings who are not able to commit to another person. There are hidden triggers in one or both people and each one struggles to survive.

Also, in this Whole-Self therapy it is discovered why some people feel or are victims in some situation. Much is that they do not realize that there are options, but as soon as they see another possibility they choose, decide, and this allows them to change or continue proclaiming that they are victims.

Our tendencies towards optimism and pessimism will be according to the experiences within the mother's womb. Therefore, the belief of whether the world is a safe place to live or is a depressing and insecure place will exist.

Anything that is said, or done, by the people in charge of supporting and witnessing the birth, at the time of birth, marks my personality!

It is my unconscious belief and self-criticism about myself. Michel Odent says: 'If a baby is not given to his mother at the time he is born, the mother is unable to be maternal and the baby is unable to be affectionate to her.'

Separating the baby from the mother is a birth trauma.

It is urgent to keep in mind that separating and isolating the baby from the mother can be traumatizing. Ideally, stay with her since she was born, take into consideration that the newborn was linked to her by the umbilical cord for 9 months. The sense of humanity is lost with this practice. The ability to feel compassion or empathy for others is affected by this procedure.

CHAPTER IV: CHILDREN IN THE FOSTER HOME

In the early 90's, I had the opportunity to train students of Educational and Clinical Psychology in a children's Foster House.

The intention was to give children a pleasant moment with music, in addition to motivating them to perform certain exercises to stimulate their physical, intellectual and emotional growth.

Likewise, for students it was a field of study in the behavior of children with abandonment syndrome regarding music and its importance in the development of children.

Music is the food of the soul.

Classes were twice a week and each psychology student devoted his attention to a little boy, doing the work that a mother does in class with her son. Companionship, support, love, motivation and encouragement.

I want to share some experiences that I had when I worked in a foster home in the city where I live, Querétaro.

David was in this house, in the nursery section because he was abandoned and collected by the Child Protection Institution. When I saw him for the first time, he was standing in the corner of the crib, not smiling, his sight lost in the distance and speechless There was no intention of establishing eye contact. I called him by his name, I put my hand on his hand; He withdrew it, he wasn't used to be touched

I was in that foster home to provide a music class once a week, to stimulate children and motivate them to interact through music. I spent a year, training educational psychologists that were doing their practices there.

David looked like an 18-month-old boy and did not walk (despite being 3 years old) he did not smile, neither trust anyone. His story is that he was picked up from where he lived, a neighbor reported the abandonment in which the child was, her mother was a prostitute and the baby did not leave his crib, from time to time she would bring him a bottle with milk so that he was fed, and that was all.

He cried a lot and that was how the neighbor realized the situation in which this little boy lived. Love, physical care and early stimulation with music made the child regain weight, become more cheerful, walked and run. Sometime after I visited them, the boy was in kindergarten and was quite sociable. I saw him crossing the yard, running with his peers, I talked to him, he approached, gave me a big smile and kept playing and running. What a difference from that David so sad and depressed that I met a time ago!

Each human being is unique and unrepeatable and when there is emotional damage it is important to seek for help, but how can you do it if you do not know that you are damaged? How to discover that the reality you live might not be your reality? How to ask for help when you are a child?

Little Mom, that was the name they gave to this 2-year-old girl who was abandoned at the gates of the foster Home, with a bag with her belongings when she was a year and a half. The only thing the girl repeated was: 'mommy, mommy'. She was 3 years old. Affectionate, she liked music, but she didn't speak, she just said: 'Mommy'.

With time and language exercises 'the mommy' began to express herself correctly and fluently. Can you imagine what this girl felt at 3 years old? loneliness, abandonment. Whatever circumstances, anything that has led the mother to leave her there, whatever! Simply, her mother THE SOURCE OF LOVE had abandoned her!

Lupita with psychomotor problems, 7 years. She was crawling around the room. The nuns commented that she really could not walk and there was no chance of giving her physical therapy for various reasons. Her legs were thin, she was generally very thin, with little muscle tone, but always smiling, she was mentally retarded, her core and arms were stronger because she was only crawling. she drooped and was wearing a bib always.

After a while, she began to pronounce a few words and the student who attended her, practically held her up with her arms to constantly motivate her to walk towards the basket of percussion instruments, because my instruction was that they would not be taken to her place, she had to move and not crawling (which was already a habit) but, getting up, even if it was in a crooked way. There were no possibilities for special devices to help the children there in the institution for obvious reasons. Lack of financial support and from my very personal point of view, several of the nuns there, were already numb to the disability of these children.

If it wasn't for the students, nobody else would had done the work we were doing. Lupita began to straighten and strengthen her legs and lift her trunk and head as much as she could.

Little by little, instead of taking her by the hands, we made her hold the sticks (wooden percussion instruments) and she was helped to walk around the room with the rhythm of the music. One day I decided that the wooden sticks would be taken away from her hands, at the time she was standing. She never stood up straight because her legs were stunted, she had them twisted towards inside. Without warning Lupita but having spoken to the girl who was attending her, I made a sign and the student released her. Lupita swayed and after 3 or 4 seconds, she dropped. We applaud her and recognize her 4 seconds of standing up by herself.

She lost a little confidence and every time she was given the wooden sticks, she clinched her hands firmly to them and did not take her eyes of the assistant's hands! but we tried again two weeks after. This time the assistant did not release the sticks slowly as the first time, quickly took them away as soon as I indicated. I was watching Lupita and according to her body language I knew when she had to be released. When she felt she was on her own, she became more aware of her posture and weight and remained more upright and for a longer time. she was taken before she fell and was recognized with applause and smiles.

After almost a year, Lupita went alone, walking awkwardly, for her percussion instruments that were used for the exercises, that was a breakthrough! several of the motor exercises were not so easy for her and she was helped out, but the best of all was that she walked on her own.

And so many cases in this place, abandonment and rejection were the main factor of these children. Situations that were not under their control, something they did not choose; there was anger and sadness in the faces of some. The music filled the hearts of these children at least 2 days a week differently and their attitudes began to change.

I stopped going home, because of my commitments to the school, but one of the students stayed training other new students who for a semester were going to do their internship there in that place. This was done for a few years and then the project was cut off because they changed the career director.

It is necessary for women to receive education on the importance of becoming mothers at all levels, not just the physical one.

CHAPTER V: THE BIRTH AND THE ORIGINS OF VIOLENCE

This leads me to remember what, on one occasion, almost 20 years ago, I read about **THE BIRTH AND THE ORIGINS OF VIOLENCE** written by the great psychologist and founder of APPPAH (Association of Prenatal / Perinatal and Health Psychology)

This is an excerpt on the subject: "**Babies Do Not Feel Pain: A Century of Denial in Medicine." by David B. Chamberlain, Ph.D** .

'There is talk of the violence that exists in the world in books, articles, conferences and in social media. People such as psychologists, teachers, police officers, politicians, theologians and people dedicated to health, feel dismayed by the increase in it and seek the origin of it at an early age of the individual, but have not gone further, to life in the womb

The violence suffered in the womb and at the time of birth is something that concerns the members of APPPAH, many of them are psychotherapists, others work in neonatal intensive care, others are in the delivery rooms and are witnesses of the violent acts suffered by these unborn babies and at the time of birth, which causes Pain in the Infant: something that Science has denied.'

There are **THE ORIGINS OF VIOLENCE** and since I met and worked with the **Psic . Jon RG Turner** and his wife **Troy GN Turner** , I could understand more thoroughly what my clients and students expressed with their positive or negative behaviors.

Turner in his method called PAM acronym that means **Prebirth Awakening Matrix (The Awakening of Prenatal Memories)** study the emotions and feelings that originate from moments before the conception of a human being! Incredible but true to understand if the conception was for violation, there we find violence in the first degree. They argue that the emotions and feelings we manifest are in the memory of our emotional DNA and have been able to verify several generations ago. It doesn't surprise me nowadays.

In ancient times and still a little over a century ago, babies were received by women: mothers, grandmothers, aunts and midwives. Entering the twentieth century doctors, usually men, began to receive babies and with this change most of the feelings, the emotions of the babies were ignored. Obstetricians and Pediatricians created painful routines that are still happening in some places.

In the year 1917 at Johns Hopkins University in Baltimore, Maryland, in the United States, investigations were conducted on whether infants felt pain. Causing tears, smiles, reactions when taking blood samples, pinches on their wrists during their sleep. Babies reacted defensively. The blood intake would be taken from the big toe and the opposite foot would hit the heel of the affected foot. The abrupt way in which they were cleaned and when carving the nape or the back of the head, made these babies wanted to flee and cried for help. Psychologist Mary Blanton concluded: "*the reflexes and instinctive reactions of newborn babies are more complex and advanced than previously thought.*"

Even with these unequivocal results, this line of experiments continued at Northwestern University and the Chicago Hospital, where newborns were stung in the cheeks, thighs and calves. The reactions of these babies grew in intensity as the days went by. It was not the same on the day they were born or the next day, then on subsequent days until the 12th. in which these tests were performed. What was not considered is that the reaction intensified over time since the mothers of these babies had received doses of anesthesia to give birth and the babies were therefore also 'anesthetized'.

The Shermans discovered that the newborn babies would cry of hunger, as well if they were released from a height of 30 to 60 cm and then they were caught, also if their heads were squeezed with some pressure just like the chin for 30 seconds. The babies tried to escape and beat with their little arms and kicked to move the objects away.

Experiments with newborns and infants continued until the 1980s, all in order to prove they felt pain. Wasn't this causing them trauma?

Unfortunately for newborns, there was the mistaken belief at that time that the immaturity of their brain did not allow them to experience, understand or remember pain.

Dr. Thomas Verny has written about **the birth and violence.** Verny states that rejection, humiliation, physical abuse and sexual abuse can turn the innocent, confident and tiny human being into an evil, cruel being and become a violent youth or adult.

<u>The way the Birth is given,
shows us the Script of Life.</u>

Many cases of criminal and violent people have been studied and a large percentage of investigations have shown that there is a relationship between complications at the time of delivery and violent behavior. (Litt 1972). There is also the hypothesis that complications at birth can damage the brain and this predisposes the child to aggressive and impulsive behavior (Mungas 1983).

Michel Odent already suggested it in 1995:

What will be the best?
PREVENT VIOLENCE or DEVELOP THE CAPACITY OF LOVING?

CHAPTER VI: VARIOUS CASES IN THE WORLD

ALLY - 27 years old

Ally is a woman who wants to emerge in her career and get one of the best jobs. She feels that her work is done efficiently but her colleagues criticized her and made life difficult for her so that she does not ascend. Ally does not know how to ignore these events and keep a firm stance because for her it is too much 'bullying' around her.

She comes to me to find out what is happening with her that she is not able to defend herself and keeps silent, she feels like a victim of these attacks, she realizes that it is not the reaction she should have, since she has yielded to impositions by her superiors.

Within the therapy she realizes that she must keep calm and ensure that harmony is not broken in her workplace, no matter how much she stops and gives in.

Nevertheless, it is not the solution for her to advance in that company. She decides to look for a new job but feels anxious that she will be rejected and takes the decision to quit, which in fact is worse. What she cannot see is that she is very efficient and in any other place she would be of great value.

When I check the prenatal memories, I find that his mother was about to commit suicide at the age of 21 because she was in an abusive relationship that was making her to become intolerant but did not expose his feelings to anyone, did not express what was happening and kept silent. A situation very similar to Ally's, shut up and tolerate. Ally's mother in those moments of her life realizes that she is pregnant with Ally and stops all suicide attempts.

Ally's father, a very controlling and manipulative 24 year old man, does not know how to relate lovingly to Ally's mother and within his history there are very hard and strict parents, so he learns that if he exercises abuse and control nobody could hurt.

Ally receives in her prenatal memory feelings of rejection, extreme vulnerability, danger, uncertainty, anxiety, abandonment, pessimism, frustration, sadness, anger, disappointment, loss of will, etc. and he experiences those feelings when she feels attacked by colleagues and practically paralyzes and does nothing, just like when she was in the womb.

She arrives at the therapy wanting to make changes and finding the root of his low self-esteem and begins to understand that she does not need abuse and that she with his promising strength is able to find a solution to this unpleasant situation.

Now she is aware of the criticisms that her mother made of herself, of the little value she felt for her, of the abuse to which she was subject and of her despair at finding no help. It is Ally, with her presence, who helps her feel alive again. Not everything is sweet as soon as Ally is born, the father is still violent and the girl grows up in that environment, does not have a good relationship with her father and that is another story to be healed for the sake of Ally.

PATTY - 40 years old

This beautiful woman has not been able to consolidate any love relationship, as she describes it by saying: 'I am making changes in myself, since I have gone through some somewhat violent and abusive relationships, one after another, the last one almost kills my spirit. I lost the baby I was expecting and there was a lot of pain. '

'I meet men who lie to me and I believe their stories because I don't like to lie, and I believe people think just like me. Now that I find Nico, I feel a great attraction to him, I don't know him in person, only online, I realized that he is a man who suffers a lot and the other day I received a message from him that disappointed me a little, he said he was going out and probably moved out and that he would stop contacting me until he came back and that it was up to me if I wanted to wait for him. He made it clear that he can only offer me his friendship, nothing more. He asked me: what do you want? and I told him that being friends would be fine because I want to have someone to talk to and hang out if possible, but this situation left me very confused. '

When I checked her prenatal life and it was very interesting to see that she was a premature baby and that she was sick for months since she was born and had to stay in the hospital.

Because of this, she has the wrong belief that she will not be able to reach her goals and that everything takes a painful time, in which others have control of her life and she is vulnerable. These memories are recycled without her knowing what was blocking her.

MARGARITA - 33 years old

Like every Wednesday at 10 in the morning, the babies' music class began, and seeing the dim morning light coming in through the window on the cushions where moms were accommodating with their babies, was one of the most pleasant views that I could have.

Margarita a beautiful young woman with white skin, shy, güerita (blondie), greenish eyes, quiet, with a smile from time to time was one my students. Her baby, beautiful girl, somewhat chubby, brunette, brown eyes and smiling. She brought her to music classes around 2 months of age. Margarita is always attentive to the class and following all the instructions on how to play the percussions instruments for the baby, very aware of how to do the exercises to stimulate her mind and body. A year had passed and each class, Margarita did her best and the baby advanced incredibly in every aspect. It caught my attention that the girl did not resemble physically either to her father or her mother, the difference was really diametral.

At that time, the year of 1998 was running in the surveys I did to people who enrolled their children in my school, they only involved personal data and the reason why they brought their children to music stimulation class. Nothing else.

And it was in that year that I met **Dr. Jon RG Turner** in a Congress that was held in the City of London in England, at Queen Mary University and another panorama was opened before my eyes of how I should closely observe certain attitudes or behaviors in my clients and their babies. In that Congress, that was entitled " Birth & Consciousness ", I also heard **Dr. David**

B. Chamberlain, Dr. William Emerson and **Dr. Thomas Verny** for the first time, to mention a few. Being these psychologists the ones that caused an impact on my desire to educate moms and babies more. Until then, my work had been very empirical and for me that congress was as if I had opened the hidden treasure chest!

Continuing with our story:...... Margarita's baby was now one year old, she approached me and told me that next week she would bring her second baby to class. I was surprised because she hadn't been pregnant yet. At that moment I realized that Margarita's firstborn was adopted, there was no other answer. I gave the information of the class where she would have to bring this second baby and asked her to make an appointment to talk more about it and to be able to do even better stimulation work with his daughters, I needed to complete a survey.

At that time, I did not have the knowledge I have today, so much of the work I did was due to my intuition and my limited knowledge about Child Psychology.

I asked Margarita in the interview: Why is it that you can't be a mom? I see that you are healthy, and you love your daughters and your husband is healthy and loves the girl.

But my concept of healthy was located only in the physical, and very little in the emotional and much less in the spiritual. Now I see everything in a holistic way and it is amazing what I can find in these women and their family upline and I now have the knowledge to support them even more in a better upbringing and even providing an intrauterine life to the unborn baby with better quality and understanding

Margarita tells me her story and says: 'I can't have children. The doctors don't know what happens because I don't have any physical impairment and my husband is fine. We had tried for a long time and it didn't happen, so we decided to adopt'.
I asked her then about her mother's pregnancy and how her birth was.

She then told me the following story: 'My mother was pregnant with me, it was her 5th. month of gestation and went on vacation to Acapulco. During the stay at the hotel, when she took the elevator to go to her room, the elevator got stuck in the 5th. floor and she stayed trapped for half an hour! She said she felt very distressed, the rest of the pregnancy and could not enjoy it anymore. When the time of delivery arrived, my mother tells me that being in the delivery room she felt fear, my birth happens and the first words that came out of her mouth were:

I WILL NEVER BE A MOTHER AGAIN!'

At that moment I understood his mental block. His mother, without any intention, installed the belief that she could not become a mother or even that giving birth was something heavy, difficult, distressing.

Within our intrauterine life and the moment of birth, everything that the mother says, experiences, lives and decrees, will be part of the emotional life of the unborn baby or the newborn.

Looking back at Margarita's case, also regarding her age, I now see that she was going through the age that is called: The age of the tests of faith.

I stopped seeing Margarita two years later, I wonder what the life of these girls would be like: they are young adults probably in their 20's . Since adopted children can go through periods in which they feel rejected, not loved, not accepted, I wonder how their lives had been. This has nothing to do with their adoptive parents, at all. This has to do with his prenatal history and his moment at birth. Something that helps to do not become so dysfunctional people is the fact of having loving adoptive parents, unfortunately when they go through these periods, even the adoptive parents themselves do not know what happens.

DIANA

A beautiful woman, mother of a baby girl who started her Musical Stimulation since she was a baby. She becomes pregnant a second time and enrolls in Prenatal Musical Stimulation classes. Mother dedicated and disciplined to the needs of her eldest daughter and taking care of her second pregnancy with the same devotion. Incomparable and devoted parents, believers and firm in their faith.

On June 14, 1994, if I remember correctly, André was born. It was not the expected birth, as it was surrounded by crisis and emergency. It was meal time, everyone in the family, including grandparents, were there and Diana begins to feel ill, lost consciousness, barely 36 weeks pregnant. A situation of preclampsia occurs . The maternal grandmother in her despair yelled at her daughter to react, shook and beat her without getting an answer, was taken to the hospital and decisions had to be made. Doctors warned relatives: the mother or the baby, who to save? Emergency surgery had to be done. The baby is born, the two survived, although they will already imagine the scene of anguish, the baby was sent to an incubator and remained there for about 3 months.

What was my intervention?

Well, I had the belief that if the voice of the parents, mainly that of the mother, was constantly heard by the baby, this would help him strengthen himself physically and emotionally, helping him go ahead. I called the parents to my school and in the small recording studio I had we recorded a cassette with the voice of Diana and her husband. I chose appropriate background music to accompany the mother's feelings and cause a positive reaction in the baby.

The nurses were very cooperative in that they disinfected the small tape recorder that went into the incubator, I remember it was wrapped in gauze and with rest periods it was there during that time and Andrés could 'feel' his mother close, listen to her voice and the encouraging words of how much he was loved and how much his parents and little sister were waiting for him at home , etc. , etc.

Andrés began to gain weight more than expected due to statistics in premature babies with this situation.

The baby suffered from pneumonia and had some difficulty breathing, also his meninges became swollen, but he got ahead like a great warrior. With this case, it is more than clear to me the goodness of the Divinity and the fact that each human being brings a short /long term mission, I don't know, but André's life has been a miracle.

I also remember on one occasion there was a client who had given birth to a child with some problems, had been born prematurely and was in an incubator, the difference between these two babies is that Andres was treated with respect and the other baby doctors gave Little hope for parents and there was even a doctor who dared to say that the baby was a human waste. So much insensitivity and arrogance that one can find in another human being who is supposedly dedicated to the mission of saving lives.

Thanks to the great love and dedication of his parents and the positive thoughts that were installed in the subconscious of that baby, his recovery was given. He is currently a successful, totally healthy young man (doctors had said he would be somehow retarded), loves life, is proactive and will soon get married.

How many human beings in emergency situations have the opportunity that Andres had?

Some even did not even have the knowledge that they could help them and that leaves a sense of failure in parents and even doctors.

This is a clear example of how, if proper precautions are taken, the individual's dysfunctional prenatal memory can be healed and even by following in the postnatal phase the necessary methods for their complete emotional recovery, which will give the individual the possibility to learn how to confront difficulties in life and acquire the desired stability to achieve personal satisfaction and good personal relationships in the future.

BETSY - 37 years old

This is a recent case. I do not know her physically, she came to me for advice, on an online chat, to be able to make decisions within her marriage that apparently is not going well at all.

This advice or consultation is done online, in the services I provide in some apps. A dreamy woman, who has the belief that everything she does has to be perfect, when we know that perfection does not exist in us or in what we do, but everything is perfectible.

Betsy married a man who tends to psychologically abuse her. Most of the time, I wonder: why people, both men and women, remain in such an abusive relationship? And the reason is because they know and understand what it is to be in situations of rejection, abuse and abuse since they were conceived, during pregnancy or at the time of delivery. Even though, most of the time they don't even know that they 'need' that adrenaline in order to survive. There comes a time when they have to realize the situation has to stop! for various reasons. That is where the transformation to a fuller life can take place. In fact, there are several occasions throughout our lives in which there are opportunities to make changes, we are simply not aware of those moments. We need help.

What is the reason why she has tolerated this behavior of her husband for 18 years? The answer is: she had not realized that he 'needed' that adrenaline. Betsy was conceived out of wedlock and her mother lived a time of anxiety and uncertainty during her pregnancy since she was not supported at that time by her partner. Then he married her. What you have to understand here is that this situation of anxiety and uncertainty affects the unborn baby because it is not being acknowledge and loved, so the unborn baby does not feel safe inside the womb.

There are many things that this pregnant woman may be saying to herself, including what she thinks of the environment around her, the people who accompany her; That internal dialogue full of positive and negative emotions, just to name a few, we have:

acceptance? rejection? loneliness? abandonment?
handicap? Conformism? restriction? crisis?
value? anger? frustration? cowardice?
curse? defeatism? disappointment? vulnerability?
trust? confusion? review? fear?
guilt? Stress? pride? cheated?
shame? anguish? abuse? fear?
faith? attack? Codependency? control?
empty? disease? selfishness? morality?
hardness? happiness? loyalty? irresponsibility?
insignificance? sweetness? protection? obsession?
purpose of life? pessimism? optimism?
resignation? relief? poverty? wealth?
social pressure? patience? intolerance?
rigidity? Self-sabotage? Sexual repression?

gratitude? violence? ugliness? toxicity?
shyness? tenderness? concern?

And I could continue with an endless list of emotions and feelings that for generations had been accumulated in the subconscious of the human being.

Betsy expresses that by analyzing this, she realizes how she has placed herself in distressing situations and now it makes sense why she does it. But her inner wisdom tells her that those emotions do not belong to her, they are the emotions, feelings or beliefs that her mother experienced. Therefore, it is time to make changes in her life.

He has 2 children, a woman and a boy. It is important that he heal his own history in order to mark a different course in the history of his children, mainly that of his daughter because as a woman it is his feminine role, in addition to the circumstances in which his daughter was conceived, how pregnancy developed and how the birth occurred.

Betsy is in a cycle of her life in which she has the need to believe in herself and in what she as a woman deserves. It is time to make the right decisions to continue evolving holistically. For this there are group and personal therapies. The internalization.

PEDRO - 40 years old

He acknowledges that he cannot trust women and it has it has been difficult for him to remain in a lasting relationship. Now married and with daughters, he realizes that he does not establish a more intimate bond with his wife and it is hard for him to interact with his daughter, although it is easier than with his wife, due to the difference in age and commitment.

Demands as a father are different from demands as a husband.

Intimating with a woman (wife) is something that scares him.

Remembering the relationship with his mother he says it is good, his mother's pregnancy was without problems. The delicate situation occurred in the delivery room. He was natural birth, at the moment the doctor received him and gave the newborn to the nurse, the nurse took him and the baby slipped and fell into the bucket! Very quickly the nurse picked him out from the bucket, but the impact and sensation are imprinted on the newborn's mind.

This action was not taken as important since the baby did not suffer physical damage, nobody at that time noticed the emotional damage, therefore, it was not restored.

Since it was a woman who didn't hold him carefully, in this case the nurse, then in his subconscious there is this idea that it is not possible to trust women because either in one way or another, they will 'leave you', or 'not support you', they 'hurt you'.

When Peter hears this analogy, he realizes his limiting belief and understands the reason for his failures in relationships and the reason for his estrangement from his wife, who in a way represents the 'nurse' in his subconscious.

Fortunately, recognizing this event as birth trauma, a special reconnection session was held with that moment and to understand that the unfortunate incident can only remain as an unfortunate memory. Accepting vulnerability to some facts is something that the human being fears for believing that there is no solution. In this case he gradually restored confidence in his wife and the women around him.

Curiously, his wife also had problems with him because she felt him distant and cold, there was little approach and she felt lonely and ignored. She did not understand the transformation in his behavior, she loved him and wanted Peter to be more affectionate.

The wife's personal history showed that her father had the same personality as Pedro and did not know how to love his daughter in the way she could feel protected.

And history was repeated!

The difference now was that they accepted the therapy to delve deeper into their situation and restore the relationship. Seeking help by mutual agreement is very healthy since both are committed to help each other and improve the relationship. The changes were seen in a short time, almost a year, struggling and having patience with themselves.

JOSÉ - 64 years old

José's story is interesting. José's mother is a woman who doesn't feel totally loved by her husband and not because he doesn't love her, but because her expectations as a woman are halfway fulfilled. She always wanted to be a mother and her first 2 babies die during pregnancy, the first at 7 months and the second at 5 months; her third pregnancy occurs and she does not realize she is pregnant, a doctor confirms that there is no such pregnancy after examining her, she becomes depressed.

Her husband tells her not to worry that they can adopt (without knowing it, she is already pregnant!) As she continues feeling a bit ill, soon she will be examined again by another gynecologist and it turns out that he confirms her she is pregnant. Her daughter is born, healthy and with that relieves her belief that she can be a mother, although the anguish is always with her. She becomes pregnant for the fourth time. Her baby daughter is just 6 months old, and this time it is José who is gestating. He is born with a weight less than 3 kg , with 9 months of gestation giving the appearance of a premature baby because it was a 'water bud' and with a cleft lip.

In those years (1953) there was not the technology and advance in science that exist today to treat these infants. Everything for José since the beginning of his life was an emergency! He was born at home and therefore did not go to an incubator. The day after his birth, his maternal grandmother and his father took him to the Capital City (since he was born in a town) to be seen by one of the 2 best pediatric surgeons at that time. His grandmother fed him with a dropper, they brought tea so that the baby would not become dehydrated.

I want you to imagine what that baby was feeling, although in the arms of his maternal grandmother, his mother, his source of love and life, could not be with him when he needed her most and instead of receiving breast milk, it was tea which in the end was not the same.

Who explained to the baby what was going on with his mother? Who explained to him what the grandmother herself and her father felt in those moments of anguish and hurry? Maybe the grandmother said something, maybe the father, for sure we don't know.

Because of his problem he could not be breastfed. The doctor who checked him said he could not have surgery until he increased his weight to at least 3 kg .

They returned to the village and the doctor who attended him suggested from the next day that he be given a drop of egg yolk daily, as well as a 'touch of chicken liver'. This baby did not develop allergies to anything.

Having 3 kgs , he had surgery to close his lip. Later the cleft palate was restructured. At 16 years of age, another nose surgery was performed and it was so traumatic for him that he no longer continued with the 4th. operation that would be a plastic surgery. I mention this, because the traumatic moments he went through in some way marked that he was not a person to conclude his projects.

Also having been 'water bud' in his prenatal memory the unborn baby lived with a bag of water that would have been a baby, therefore 'lived' next to an unfinished project.

I want you to visualize the picture. The mother with a 13-month-old girl, her baby José in this situation and with special care regarding her diet and care. Surrounded by love for the family without a doubt, but no one who explains to the baby his condition (something that I suggest to future parents today, is that since they want to conceive a child, they will talk and receive it with love).

José turns out to be a very smiley baby and has his difficult moments, because of his problem he needs more attention, but his mother becomes pregnant again when he is barely 4 months old. Now we have a young mother of around 24 years of age with an 18-month-old baby girl, a 4-month-old baby with a cleft lip and pregnant again!

How much does this woman have to divide herself in order to give the necessary attention to each of her children? and what about herself? She states that this situation did not worried her because it was 'normal' at that time to be 100% dedicated to the children accepting the situation as it was and without so many questions.

Definitely another perspective of life.

What I want you to realize is how the family environment in equilibrium is of the utmost importance for parenting. An extraordinary workload for both the physical and emotional mother is not recommended for a healthy holistic development in the infant. The situation is that José not only had those two siblings, his mother continued to get pregnant and losing babies, therefore, he had an anxious, nervous, worried mom, working hard and tired. Worse, with an irresponsible husband who had an extramarital relationship, of which this woman had knowledge, so there was no true love with her husband.

As a therapist I am, a common denominator in my clients is feeling unloved. That is your perception, that is your reality and it is not disputed. In certain circumstances they are actually alone, they have expectations of how the love given to them should be. They grow up with the belief that they will not find love or that love is not for them and in case they have someone loving them, they will always question and challenge them to prove that they really cannot be loved!

And all this has to do with trauma before birth or at birth. In addition to this, in case of physical disabilities, this feeling of abandonment and lack of love intensifies.

José developed as a nervous, sympathetic and shy child to some extent. His childhood and adolescence lived with his siblings and parents within a general acceptance family, his father was not much a guy that would go out on his own just with his sons to share walks or movies or sports; he was a father who worked constantly and most of the upbringing was done by his mother.

His speech therapies were the corrections that his own older sister made to pronounce the words well, since at that time there were no speech therapists and in his teens his performance at school was not the best.

He did not finish his Law studies, he was very friendly and always sought the acceptance of the group and did not consolidated anything. In his young adulthood he got pregnant a young woman whom he had met one day in a park, he didn't see her anymore until he received the call that he had become a father and as a consequence decided to marry her and quit the University

How could José's life have been different?

One theory is restoring the mother / child bond since birth, as that didn't happen, it would have been viable in childhood or adolescence. But in those years no one knew about this. The mother did what she could, what she knew, and what her intuition told her. Today we have more knowledge and alternatives to support pregnant mothers and newborns offering a better quality of life in all aspects.

Something wonderful is that women are recovering the lead of her power to decide how she wants her pregnancy to develop and how she wants her baby to be born in order to become a more balanced and happy human being.

ALANA - 46 years old

Alana comes to inquire about whether it will be possible for her to divorce on good terms, since her husband for about 23 years has been unfaithful and has left her for the woman with whom he had a relationship of almost a year.

Alana is afraid that she cannot establish a love relationship with someone else, she is afraid of rejection and there is a 56-year-old gentleman, divorced 5 years ago and to whom she is attracted to. This man does not speak much, he is sensitive and very cautious in the way he addresses to her.

Somehow this gentleman has certain attitudes that her first husband also has; Alana doesn't want to fall into a relationship where she could get hurt again. As I delve deeper into her story, I realize that her fear of being abandoned does not begin with her first husband but in her gestation.

When I check her emotions and blockages, I found out that something happened that does not allow her to trust men and it turns out that her father accused his mother of being pregnant with a child (in this case she) that was not his! Alana somehow remembers that her mother didn't loved her very much and her father was an alcoholic.

Sadly, in her childhood the father forced her to drink when she was 5 years old and her mother became furious, Alana remembers that apparently in that drunken state her father abused her by touching her inappropriately.

She is the second of 3 women and comments that her sisters also remember something similar. Alana starts drinking at age 10.

Her father, a 73-year-old man is selfish, authoritarian, controlling and has maintained his marriage for 50 years despite the difficulties with Alana's mother, it seems that they are made for each other. the mother has a strong and very controlling personality, both parents have no confidence in themselves and constantly fight.

In her father's story, he says, there is a lot of pain. When he was 4 years old, he suffered burns due to a fire in his house, at age 12 he no longer supports his parents' relationship and leaves the house to live on his own. From there we can see the trajectory of dysfunctionality that exists in his family and having no help, he repeats the story with his wife, Alana's mother.

Alana feels unloved and used. She gets married to a man who somehow believes she will give him the stability she needs, he had already had a previous relationship, and a son from that relationship. what Alana did not say is if he divorced or only separated. Her first husband's son is a 26-year-old boy who has strong emotional problems and is in trouble with society.

From this marriage are born a son, a daughter and twins (boys). The young man is 23 years old and is a loving son, very attentive to his mother and who needs to develop much more self-confidence. His middle daughter is 19 years old. She is a girl who helps others, something insecure and has a hard time expressing her deepest thoughts.

Alana becomes pregnant 14 years ago with twins and intends to abort them, changes her mind and they are born prematurely.

Currently they are boys who challenge the authority a lot and who do not know how to treat their mother with kindness and respect, somehow even though she has done her best as a mother, they have printed in her prenatal memory the desire she had to get rid of them, and this is an attack on their persona.

Therefore, not only with their mother, but they will have that problem of relating to women because they represent danger in their subconscious.

What is needed is that the boys (twins) have supportive therapy to reconcile their appreciation for women and also because they are going through a situation beyond their control, which is the separation of their parents, and the abandonment of the father mainly. In an age when they need an honest father figure and there is none.

Alana needs to strengthen her self-esteem in her since with the situation of abuse in different grades and styles, she will continue without trusting men and it will be difficult to build a positive and healthy love relationship.

ADRIENNE - 47 years old

In Adrienne's first consultation, a Cognitive Profile is performed. One of the most important images is the one that opens his analysis: the one that represents the pain the unborn baby experiences at birth to rejection, abandonment and high risk.

His story is that she was not conceived with love, she was not expected. At the time she announced that she was ready to be born (this is the first contraction her mother felt), her father was not present, mother begins labor, the mother arrived to the hospital and her husband met her there and when the nurses received the woman, took her on a stretcher inside the hospital and Adrienne was born on the stretcher. In that moment his father caught her in the air. Note that this represents a very strong adrenaline load due to the impact of the sensation of falling.

She does not remember that her father had been lovingly to her and unfortunately throughout her childhood she suffered from sexual abuse by an older man between 35 and 40 years old.

This happens when she was 9 years old, she feels very guilty because she says she liked what her body felt; she and her sisters knew this person since he was one of their neighbors and her mother used to entrust the girls to her care when she had to leave, therefore, they trusted him until this situation occurred and she stopped him and allowed that it happened so that he did not do the same to his sisters, The man of course asked him to keep 'his secret'.

Apparently, this situation lasted about 3 years. The risk, the fear, the anguish, the loneliness, the pain, all this adrenaline burden is present and does not know who to trust.

When she is 17, she also suffered another person's abuse and feels guilty again. She comes to the office because she is thinking about divorcing since her husband has no interest in her, nor does she; They have talked about this situation of no physical approach and there is doubt in it that he also had an extramarital relationship with another person.

Adrianne has been in an extramarital relationship for 6 years, (again a risk situation) and said that even the person with whom she has this relationship was not to her liking and that she has kept it going for having sex; little by little he has fallen in love with this man and now he is asking her to live with him and for that she would have to divorce. She has two children: an 18-year-old girl and a 17-year-old boy. Her husband has been out of work for 3 - 4 months and so it seems he does not make the effort to find something, is dedicated to playing video games and there is a situation of coldness in the house.

She has expressed to him her decision to separate and he does not want to leave the family home arguing that it belongs to him. What distresses her most, in this moment, is that her son is annoyed with her because of the decision she intends to make.

After she came with me, the children came separately and the husband as well. The husband in his analysis showed that he had no extramarital relationship. He said that he loves her and that he feels very distressed by the lack of work, before they got married he had a stable job and after the marriage he couldn't stay in a job more than 2 or 3 years. He is currently thinking of taking a job outside the city just to get away from home and only have separation without divorce. He feels diminished by her.

He does not know about his wife's extramarital relationship and feels that it is not the same as before. He loves his children, but he has not known how to be a loving father and he recognizes this fault.

Their children expressed in the analyzes that they need more paternal presence, they are certain of the conflicts in the home.

The boy senses that his parents could divorce and in fact he told his mother that if they decide to separate one day, they would not put him in the dilemma of deciding with whom he was living with.
The girl senses that her mother has an extramarital relationship but does not express it openly and does not speak of a possible separation, but she herself cannot relate well with young people of her age.

Here it is very clear how the case of a rejected and then ignored baby, without loving basis on the part of his parents, is easy prey to abuse (in search of affection and acceptance). Establishing a relationship with another being that will ignore and reject because it is a behavior that is well learned.

Then looking for an emotional relationship of risk (as was the abuse of small) and all this very well planted in the subconscious.

We are also talking about someone who has not had prenatal therapeutic help to understand all this behavior development before life and the couple. And so he could continue the story with his children if adequate measures are not taken to heal his prenatal and childhood memories.

ELISA - 32 years old

This woman, of Italian descent, was the mother of a very intelligent child. The mother's appearance was not very healthy. She had a lot of burden from the family, her son was very talented and her husband was sick, suffered from fibromyalgia.

She constantly looked depressed, smiled little, did not care much for her appearance, extremely thin, to the extent that I thought she was anorexic. In fact, I asked her about her health on one occasion and she told me that everything was fine, only tired of her husband's illness and the demands of work and being a mother. She was white, dark, tall and super skinny, finally one day I decided to ask her about her birth.

Great was my surprise when telling her story!

She had been a twin, but her twin failed to develop because she was mummified.

Yes, what you read! He mummified!

Apparently, the doctors said the double pregnancy never realized, since Elisa was positioned exactly on the other baby. This may have been around the 1960s, when ultrasound was not yet available. The mother, it seems, never reported feeling bad. Elisa says that at the end of her mother's pregnancy, she had a caesarean section; they take Elisa from her mother's womb and find the other mummified baby below her.

Elisa doesn't mention if her mother felt bad, she said nothing about it. She commented only that throughout her life she has always felt that something is missing and mentions that she somehow carried a 'fault' that she did not understand.

When these situations occur, there is a tendency for the person to seek to restore the 'damage' done by supporting others at the expense of their own health, as was the case with her sick husband, who had to spend a lot of time in bed and she taking care of him , soon the husband passed away and she became a widow with her baby to take care of.

It underwent an amazing transformation without the 'burden' of the sick husband. She began to recover gaining enough weight to look better and I noticed with the passage of time, she was more smiling. She attended supportive therapy because she subconsciously 'carried a blame' for not being able to help the husband either.

What I then observed due to her history and appearance was the physical congruence with the story. It was like honoring the loss of the being that was next to her and that was not achieved, a mirror in which she saw herself inside the mother's womb, and her physical representation to 'see' her pregnant partner.

When she understood where her mood came from, in some way, she also allowed her husband to leave and not be tied to a disease that ultimately led him to the grave.

ADELA - 25 years old

25-year-old Adela was afraid of getting pregnant and didn't know the reason since she and her husband felt a huge desire to be parents. Two failed pregnancies saddened her. For no reason, supposedly, since she was a healthy woman.

In her genetic emotional memory were the miscarriages that her own mother had suffered before her birth. Adela had developed in what is called a toxic uterus. Our cells have memory, the uterus that has suffered voluntary or involuntary losses is called toxic womb. Therefore, the baby that is being developed in a toxic womb 'feels' loneliness and anguish due to the previous 'failure'.

That baby who is born under these conditions and is not explained by what is happening, is born with the belief that to achieve goals in life are difficult, have their risks, that at times there is loneliness and fear, there is uncertainty and doubt when reaching the end of a project. It is then where the mother-child bond therapy should occur, since there is knowledge of pregnancy, expressing acceptance and love for it, talking with the unborn baby, sending messages of hope and faith, encouragement and strength.

When working with this method of Musical Prenatal Stimulation, pregnancy is lived in a more positive and joyful way. Ideally, after the losses, a healing session of the mother's womb will take place, and grief will be experienced for as long as necessary, each woman is different. As soon as she is ready to seek pregnancy again, in this way the desired baby will be gestated in a healed, restored uterus, a mother more confident, physically, emotionally and spiritually strengthened.

MIRIAM - 21 years old

Miriam, single mother, drug addict. You get pregnant and realize your pregnancy 3 months later. Apparently, she stopped taking drugs. When Miriam registered her baby in the nursery that I had, (the baby was about 8 months old) she had prolonged crying periods, sometimes a quiet cry, sometimes in full scream; then there were changes, she was totally silent, angry, annoyed, this could be seen in her face, in her gestures, in her behavior.

She tended to hit, stain and throw things. She rejected food sometimes. Her behavior was so variable, she was moody. The mother was totally disconnected from her. The maternal grandmother was the one who worried about having what was necessary, although both were going to leave and pick up the girl from school.

I did not know that the mother had used drugs, I was not reported. The girl went to the nursery because her mother did not take care of her, the grandmother worked out of home and the baby girl showed apathy. They wanted me to help her socialize with other children too.

When I noticed the mood swings in this baby, I called Grandma and then asked her about her daughter's pregnancy, childbirth, etc. I knew she was a single mother. When the grandmother told me that she had used drugs and was an alcoholic, I understood. There was extreme rejection and supposedly the mother was already 'clean' from her addiction, but she didn't get involved in a loving way with the girl and vice versa.

When the girl began walking, she would go wherever she wanted and usually ignored the instructions. At first, I allowed this, knowing that much restriction would not be good for her.

She was free to go here or there in the nursery (there were a few children) and the garden was huge. The girl had the freedom to explore, smiled more, but assaulted her classmates again and again. Scratched, bit, kicked, etc.

She could be considered a violent girl and on the other hand she began to change her behavior, smiling much more and being nice, but the contrasts in behavior were diametral.

The mother was invited to participate in the music classes to have a closer approach with the baby, her disposition was initially reluctant, little by little she became more and more involved. Grandma told me that when Anita was born, she experienced a detoxification process and it had been difficult for the baby. It was understandable because her behavior and her reaction to others was defensive. For her, the slightest indication of discipline was taken as an assault on her.

In addition to this there was the rejection of the mother. Fortunately, there was the grandmother. Anita gradually transformed her behavior, surrounded by love, acceptance, affection, music and art.

The girl left the nursery at 5 when she went to the Kindergarten. Recently I saw her become a teenager, 13 years old. she has a baby brother, his mother got married. We talked for a few minutes, apparently her life is more stable. Anita seemed fine, and I say it seemed because again I saw that gesture of disgust that characterized her for a long time as a baby. Unfortunately, I lost track of her, I didn't know about them anymore.

It is well known that the children of drug addicted parents have some probabilities to create the same addiction to these substances as their parents. They can go through a detoxification treatment, but they suffer too much.

It is important that women are aware that gestating a baby in good health is very important. It is good you create an awareness of respect for the beginning of a life. It is known that babies suffering from maternal rejection can become criminals, also those babies who have been separated from their mother due to emergency procedures.

These situations contribute to the development of an attitude of coldness and anger towards life and others. There is evidence that babies who have not had a close relationship with any human being who truly loves them, are those who show a lack of compassion and understanding for others, there is a risk that they are antisocial and develop psychological and psychiatric problems.

These human beings with antisocial disorders are extremely vulnerable. They started their life without creating a bond of love with their mother, so they rebel before the authority, they find it hard to establish lasting relationships with others.

They cannot believe that they can be sincerely loved and sometimes they are cruel, they hurt without feeling remorse or guilt, they cannot empathize, they do not trust others; They can become teenagers who attempt suicide once or several times.

Depending on how quickly the appropriate therapy is offered and carried out, this memory of rejection can be change to a belief of acceptance of oneself and b others to achieve more balanced life.

LINA - 40 years old

Lina, a 40-year-old woman who doubts a lot about her abilities. She is a trainer of new voluntary elements to help resolve legal situations in a complaint office of a sports development in the city where she lives.

She is a divorced mother, with three children and believes that she needs a husband to be able to get ahead and continue her studies in Law. The work she has is not 100% satisfying, although it is not something that totally displeases her, but she feels that she can give more and that there she is not giving her full potential. In the therapy session when I asked about her birth, she tells me that she was born three weeks before the expected day, being a premature girl with a mother who did not pay much attention to her and a father who was caring for her as much as he could.

She grows with the idea that in order to go ahead in life with your dreams, you need a man in the house; she is currently wanting to take the decision of changing jobs, continue studying law, but she immediately sabotages herself saying she cannot do it because she has three children to attend.

Some courses can be taken online, other trainings have to be live, face-to-face, in the end she needs to change that limiting belief that she has regarding the need to have a partner to support her and continue her studies since she has the talent for that career and what blocks her is the insecurity that she feels due to the prenatal experience that the goals are not achieved, also says that the relationship with her mother is not good but due to her mother's personality, something that she does not consciously realize that she is quite similar to her mother. When her mother was pregnant with her, she had 3 abortion attempts, she bled a lot, but in the end, hopefully Lina was born prematurely.

FERNANDA - 16 years old

Fernanda, a teenager who arrives at the music school to learn guitar. His mother attends early musical stimulation classes with his 3-year-old brother. Fernanda is the daughter of a single mother since she was abandoned by the man who got her mom pregnant and never took responsibility for his actions.

Fernanda's mother lived in the paternal house when she gave birth. Grandma did not accept her completely. During pregnancy, Fernanda's mother felt loneliness and sadness. She gave birth to her daughter and apparently continued studying and working, therefore, she had to leave her in the care of the grandmother. Unfortunately, the grandmother was very intolerant, and the baby had to stay in her room all the time.

As she grew up, the mother says that the girl's behavior tended to be good, but she was not allowed to leave the room because the grandmother did not want to have a mess in the house. The girl once painted the walls and door of the room. She practically lived cloistered. Weekends were different because mom was at home.

The mother married a good man, who adopted Fernanda and life took a huge turn, changing completely for good. Despite this, Fernanda, in her teens begins to give obedience problems, is lazy in school and fights with her mother a lot. The adoptive father talks a lot with her, but she is closed to listen to any advice.

One day the mother asks me for an appointment with Fernanda. Fernanda had made changes in the way she dressed, dyed part of her hair in purple and was starting to physically hurt herself. One day the mother found her cutting her wrists from her arms. She was not successful in her suicide attempt. The alarm was beginning to ring for mom.

Fernanda had a study called Cognitive Profile Analysis, created by Vivian John Crowhurst, a painter and therapist. This method is impressively beautiful (which I will write in another chapter to explain the benefits it brings to the human being), in a graphic way through symbols and images, we can find out what the subconscious of the individuals harbors and find if there are blockages from the prenatal phase of their lives and what is the potential they have to excel in their lives.

The Profile showed that Fernanda was very angry with her mother and that she always felt at risk. There was physical abuse in her prenatal memory as well. The mother then commented that one of the reasons why Fernanda's father also left them, was because she asked him to end the relationship, because there was physical violence, he beat her while she was pregnant.

Although Fernanda did not know her biological father, she had knowledge of physical abuse since being in the womb: she experienced it, lived it, felt it.

This abuse comes to mind when she feels not understood and ignored. Therefore, in this very important change in life that is adolescence, the experience sprang back into his memory.

The mother really did not know how to handle this situation since she thought it was only hormonal changes, the root was in prenatal life.

A music therapy session was held to create a mother's/daughter bond as the first step. I will talk about this type of sessions with music in another chapter of the book, about the benefits of music from the prenatal stage to 6 years. In this type of session, the individual recognizes that the external circumstances that damaged them were not under their control and they are helped to understand this to alleviate the relationship with the parents and their relationship with themselves.

Then he took a self-esteem course for young people for 6 months alternated from time to time with some individual therapy. Here also what contributed to Fernanda's recovery was the fact that there was a lot of cooperation between her adoptive father and her mother and interest in her getting ahead.

For a while she took guitar lessons. She began her high school and focused on it.

Fernanda is currently married, her physical appearance changed completely, she looks full and happy and has a child.

ANABEL - 32 years old

Anabel, mother of a 4 year old girl, student of my music class. Anabel had been 2 years attending music classes with her daughter. Everything apparently was fine. After some time, the mother approached me to express that she was worried about her daughter's behavior. She was wondering if I had not noticed changes in her daughter and if her behavior in the classroom was adequate, to which I answered yes, her behavior was adequate, and I did not really have problems with her. Her performance was excellent as always.

Surprised the mother for my answer, she began to cry.

Anabel owned a business in the city downtown and despite the responsibility she and her husband had, her little girl was always well taken care of. I was surprised then to see the mother so worried. His story was as follows: 'I am scared because my daughter is telling me and repeating every so often that why I wanted to kill her when she was in my belly'.

It was then that I learned the story of her pregnancy. Everything was going well. Wanted baby, planned, with loving and responsible parents. It happened that once they had gone for a holiday during the weekend, Anabel was 5 months pregnant. On the way back to the city, Anabel's husband lost control of the car due to another driver who made a dangerous maneuver in a bend and Anabel's car crashed into a tree. As soon as Anabel, who was in the passenger seat, realized the danger and saw that they were going against the tree, she instinctively raised her legs in a fetal position to protect her belly.

You can imagine the adrenaline rush that this woman had at that time.

She hit her knees against the dashboard of the car and broke them. Everything else is history, the ambulance arrived, they were picked up, taken to the hospital, Anabel's knees are broken, and her pregnancy continues in bed to recover: the baby is fine. All in order!

At least that seemed to be what they believed. because one thing was to check that the baby was physically well, but it never occurred to anyone that this baby was emotionally scared and confused.

Her sanctuary, the mother's womb, had suffered a huge adrenaline rush, just like herself!

But no one has taught us to react in these moments of emergency, in case of being pregnant, towards what is happening to the baby and how to speak to them; because everything happens so quickly.

The attention was mainly for Anabel, not for the baby, however the baby was inside and well. And his emotions? And what did the baby feel? Fortunately, there was still time to heal that memory of anxiety and anger. On one occasion I read that at 4 years the prenatal memories are recycled, so in some cases behavior changes in children.

Mom Anabel did a special music therapy session to restore her mother's bond with her daughter and the girl's attitude began to change, the unpleasant moment of the crash was not mentioned again. It has been proven that some babies can 'see' what happens in the mother's womb and outside of it, experiments of following a light have shown eye movement of the unborn baby. When they are seen by ultrasound in what an amniocentesis test is done, babies move to the side when they see the needle penetrating the mother's womb.

CHAPTER VII: BIRTH TRAUMA

There is much to talk about what the BIRTH TRAUMA is, and from the prenatal phase.

Sigmund Freud, father of Psychoanalysis, said that the likely source of anxiety symptoms presented by his clients, may be due to his experiences lived at birth, unfortunately he himself did not support the idea much because his personal beliefs were based on the brain at birth the baby was not mature. Therefore, he preferred to think that trauma was a fantasy created by his clients.

Otto Rank, a student of Sigmund Freud, was convinced of the existence of birth trauma and was passionately dedicated to building a form of psychoanalysis that was directed directly at birth. (Written on Birth Trauma 1924).

Freud rejected this theory. Some psychotherapists today support Rank's theory.

About this topic, in Connections Primary by Elizabeth Noble (1993), The New Primal Scream by Arthur Janov (1991), The Holotropic Mind of Stanislav Grof (1992) and Lynda Share, If Someone Speaks, it Gets Lighter: Dreams and the Reconstruction of Infant Trauma (1994).

If it is still believed that the brain of an unborn child is immature or even when newborn, this will continue to be a major obstacle to the progress in the understanding of babies. Even so, we must be more careful in how we care for pregnant women and how we receive babies in this world, knowing that they are human beings, not a 'product' or object.

Fortunately in this 21st century there are already many people in various health fields talking about the need to modify the way pregnant women and their unborn babies are treated, as well as to prepare a healthy environment for the reception of a new life, a new being that translates into a new society.

There are many factors that can be considered as Birth Trauma, many of them are not in the control of women whether they are unaware of the issue or that another person takes control of the birth of their child.

Today there is enough information about natural birth, to ensure that the baby is born in the best emotional health conditions.

Parents are invited to have the responsibility of creating an environment conducive to receiving that new being, which in turn depends entirely on the decisions of this pair of adults who will function as their earthly parents.

The peace of the world begins in the womb. If what we want is to live in peace and harmony, let us take care of that sanctuary called the womb.

CHAPTER VIII: THE EFFECTS ON THE NEWBORN IN THE EMERGENCY ROOM

Sometimes it has been necessary for newborns or premature babies to be taken to the emergency room where they need special care due to problems that arise at the time of birth.

There are endless situations that can take these babies to incubators. Whatever the cause are moments of stress, pain and confusion for the little ones. There are institutions that have really dedicated and sensitive staff to treat them, and there are others in which the staff has simply 'disconnected' from the pain to assist them. There is every kind of people, I do not like to generalize. Unfortunately, despite the generous care of some nurses, they are not all trained in how to talk to babies about the procedures that are being carried out in them to help them breathe better, gain weight, monitor their heart, feed them , etc...

We know that, as necessary as it may be, it is an invasion of your person. The baby is so vulnerable that everything really bothers him, the probes through his nose or mouth, the position in which he must be in order to be 'manipulated' (as some express) according to the needs at that time.

That is the word **MANIPULATED**!

Something he or she will detect promptly and rebel against it. There is a way to heal these memories with therapies to restore the mother / child bond.

KATIE - 37 years old

Katie is divorced and now she is in a romantic relationship with a 40-year-old man who is very hardworking, intelligent and caring. She frequently doubts whether their relationship will be lasting. She has a teenage daughter and a baby of almost 2 years. Her partner fails to understand why she is silent or upset when she talks about projects to be carried out in which he asks for her help or suggests what she could contribute.

Checking her past, she says she comes from a family without serious problems. The mother's pregnancy was good, there were no implications. The mother's desire was to have a home birth and that it would be calmer in this way. The doctors did not accept his idea and gave birth in a hospital. The doctors spent the time telling her everything she had to do and not do. The labor lasted more than 10 hours, she was the firstborn. Her father did not support his mother in her wish for her daughter to be born at home. According to Katie's comments, her dad was always a passive man.

Her mother resents not being able to be in control of the birth as she wanted it. Looking back, that happens to Katie today. There are situations in the relationship that escape control and that bothers her. She feels that a certain rhythm is imposed when she wants to go at her own pace. She has had in the past and even today, problems with accepting an authority. Remember that doctors represent authority and however she remembers their imposition on their mother's decisions. Mom's stress led her to have a very long birth. No wish of the mother was respected. That's why she avoids getting involved.

JESS - 31 years old

Jess wonders what she can do to improve her communication with the people she works with. Creative and talented, attractive woman. More recently she has felt segregated from the group, which creates anxiety in her and a feeling of not being good enough for the job she does. This has led her to work on her own. She is a musician and works teaching private lessons.

What really happens is that she doubts her abilities and that makes her look like an uncertain person with little confidence for the work to be developed.

When talking about her mother's pregnancy, she expresses that her mother went through very difficult times when she was pregnant. Her mother was 35 years old and her father 39. He was diagnosed with esophageal cancer and her father died in January 1986 leaving a bereaved widow and an unborn baby. The mother in her duel, with great burden of loneliness and anger at the circumstances in which she was, gives birth before term.

Jess is born in March 1986, with 2 weeks left to complete her time in the womb, therefore she is considered premature. The prenatal memories of this woman are not entirely encouraging, there is loss, abandonment, illness, sadness, fear of the future, confusion, loneliness. Let's keep in mind that those are her mother's emotions that have been drunk in the form of chemicals through the umbilical cord through her body and therefore she has believed them as her own.

She also comments that she had 4 suicidal attempts and 7 emergency hospitalizations in psychiatric hospitals, one of them was due to postnatal depression. She is a survivor.

Now she understands that the fact that no one explained to her about the loss of her father at the time when she was in her mom's womb and no emotional support, is why in many situations today she feels that she is not welcome, that it is easy to reject her, and not consider her so that brings confusion.

While remembering the death of her father, Jess explains that there is a phrase that her mother told her dad when he was already very ill. The mother told him: "It's okay to let go of everything, it's good to let go, it's good to leave."

She did this by following the instructions of a nurse who suggested that she do it so that her husband felt good and that she was able to move on while he was there, and in case he died everything would be fine. It was like giving him permission to die since the father was very worried about them. The father was only 39 years old.

The situation is that the unborn baby, my client Jess, heard what her mother was saying and could not tell if the message was for her or someone else.

Jess married a violent and addicted man, when in difficult moments of his life, Jess came to think that there was no problem if she died, someone would have to take care of her daughter, and the girl would be better off without her there. The most intense suicide attempt was in 2012 when her daughter was 4 years old.

She separated from this man and joined another one with the same characteristics in personality. She had a daughter with him and continued to suffer from domestic violence and drug addiction.

In 2016 Jess tries again to commit suicide, but this time it was much more traumatic. This was in the days before his 30th. birthday.

She was in a difficult situation, in a relationship of domestic violence and the child protection social services withdrew her daughter from her because of addiction problems as well.

On that occasion she was admitted to a rehabilitation center for drug addicts, from the month of August 2016 to the month of January 2017. It was a very restrictive place, she could not express as she had wanted, they provided medications for people with mental problems, and she was more stressed than ever. There was no physical contact, they were not allowed, not even hugs between them, they had to take care of the language they used; she was in that place because the lawyer suggested that she should be hospitalized so that she could see her daughters, otherwise she would be restricted and away from them.

The youngest girl, her 2-year-old daughter, was adopted by a family with 4 children. She is the youngest, she is in good hands and this is called an open adoption because they allow the birth mother to be in contact with her. It also turns out that the adoptive father is the uncle of the biological father of the baby, in this way the baby is not away from her biological family.

The adoptive mother and 3 of the siblings suffer from a disease called ' pompe disease ', it is a rare and progressive congenital disease (transmitted from parents to children), which affects the muscles and can occur in babies, children or adults. In people with Pompe disease , sugar builds up in the muscles causing the muscles to become damaged. The most common symptoms are:

- Muscular weakness.
- Poor muscle tone
- Enlarged liver
- Insufficient growth and height.
- Trouble breathing.
- Feeding problems
- Infections in the respiratory system.
- Ear problems

Therefore, this family is also used to attending rehabilitation therapies, they know how to be empathic and somehow Jess feels calm that her daughter will be well taken care of.

Jess told me that now she understood why every time she tried to commit suicide, she saw it as a solution to end the pain she was experiencing at the time, and it didn't cause her regret to make that decision. In his subconscious were his mother's words addressed to his father when he was so sick: 'IT IS OK TO RELEASE'.

Her therapy is carried out to strengthen her self-confidence. Let go of those emotions that don't belong to her and embrace who she really is. Due to her mother's duel over her father's death, she did not count on her 100% as she was trying to understand the situation.

Jess does not know how to ask for help since she was not breastfed either and being breastfed allows us to have confidence and accept the support that others can give us. She segregates alone from the groups, assumes that they will reject her and causes the rejection. Suicide attempts are manifested as a means of attracting attention and somehow a 'punishment' for being 'the cause of your mother's sadness'. That happens in the newborn's mind when there is a loss of this species.

ANNE -25 years old

She has not been able to trust any man. Relating in general is difficult for her. The maternal grandmother raised her. Her mother became pregnant while she was single and when she gave birth in the hospital, she abandoned her there. The Institution's staff found the maternal grandmother and she went to pick up the baby. Nothing was known about the mother.

We understand this as a pregnancy of uncertainty and little acceptance. Anne keeps asking herself today why? What was wrong with her that her mother didn't loved her? She also knew that she came from a dysfunctional family in which the grandfather had not been the male support figure expected in a home. The grandmother had been a widow, but her daughter had left home as a teenager, joined bands and eventually became pregnant with Anne.

Lack of love, immaturity, commitment, ignorance; Call him what you want, the result is an abandoned baby.

Anne is single, does not believe in men, she has trust issues as well with women. This is sad, because mothers represent the source of love and life. Unable to trust even women, Anne somehow denies herself. The grandmother raises her, we agree that she loves her, the fact is that the grandmother also suffers from depression because of the loneliness she is in and the sadness of not knowing about her daughter, Anne's mother. Therefore, the surrounding environment is not the healthiest. Depression and abandonment.

Anne will require therapy to be able to understand all this and accept that none of these emotions belong to her. She will learn to know herself, to see her own beauty and to resurface as a healthy and happy woman.

ROSA - 7 years old

There are also cases with positive resolutions. Rosa is born in good health, she has been an expected, desired, planned baby. The pregnancy was healthy. On the second day of life, while still in the hospital, waiting for her father to take them home, their life suddenly changes. Instead of the father coming to pick them up, he arrives as a patient, to the emergency room of the same hospital, having suffered a massive heart attack and dies that same day.

The mother receives the news and her grief begins. But they have a lovely family. Maternal grandparents immediately prepare to help their daughter and granddaughter.

The paternal grandparents were also there and somehow the tragedy did not allow the love with which she was expected to be overshadowed by the loss of their father. Despite the sadness of the mother, the girl at no moment feels rejected, the grandfather immediately becomes the male figure for her.

When older, the girl begins to ask if her father will return? She never met him and doesn't understand death and perhaps with the time passing by, she will understand better that this is not possible, she knows him by pictures that mom has kept with her and begins to accept his physical absence. There are pictures of him with her mother being pregnant. Those are her memories.

She has grown in a healthy way, her attitude towards life is positive, she now knows how her father's death happened and she has accepted it naturally. She was never treated as a victim for not having her biological father present, the love her father felt for her was transmitted to her when Mom was pregnant of her, and how she was desired by both. It was explained, within the beliefs of the family, how it was his time to leave and be in the presence of the Divine.

SARA - 5 years old

Sara's mother tried to abort when she was in the second month of pregnancy, despite this the baby remained stayed alive. Her mother's partner did not want to have a baby and as soon as she knew she was pregnant, he left her. In her frustration and sadness, she made the decision to abort her, as it didn't work the first time, she made a second attempt on the third month, and it didn't work out either. Anyway, the pregnancy continued, but the mother was dissociated from her baby, did not speak to her and she gestated without being loved.

She was born healthy but came out to be a fuzzy baby. When the mother sees her, she worries and begins to take better care of her, the girl has a cold and distant behavior towards the mother in general, there are good moments and her relationship is bearable until, at 4 and a half years, she is reported from the nursery that Sara is saying that when she was very young her mother wanted to kill her, the girl was aggressive with her classmates.

The mother explains to the director that lately she has had some problems with the girl due to her rebelliousness to eat or obey the simplest instructions, but she is only told off, she does not hit her, she does not mistreat her, she does not yell at her. Mom can't believe the story of her daughter. The principal suggests that the girl should go to therapy because her story seems to be very convincing.

The mother shows up with Sara, 5 years old, in my office. I analyze the subconscious of the girl through a cognitive profile therapy method (CIP). The result shows that the girl knows that Mom wanted to abort her when she was in her womb.

How is it possible for such a little girl to know? When she chose the card that symbolizes the loss of a baby, I asked her why she had chosen it and she replied: that is how I was little when Mom wanted to kill me.

The mother was present, so I didn't have to say more. Just imagine the mother's face! I continued with the analysis by letting her see that the girl had felt very lonely and confused (without adding more wood to the fire) and could not know that she, Sara, felt lonely as well and that when she was born she had to learn to love her.

I did not delve into the girl's analysis because it was not convenient or necessary, the interpretation was then done alone for the mother, I explained more deeply all the facts. It is impressive how depending on the trauma we can remember our intrauterine lives.

The mother and Sara came a second time for a therapy called: mother & child bonding with music. That kind of therapy is done when the baby is in a hypnotic moment, then the mother expresses her fears she had during pregnancy and talks about other things with her, each person is different, therefore, the therapies have to be different, The music is selected carefully accordingly to their personalities, is quite personalized.

Sara's behavior began to change and the mother's attitude toward her too.

CHAPTER IX: MY OWN HISTORY

I studied for becoming a Trilingual Accountant Secretary in a renowned school in Mexico City, Sao Martin School, it was exclusively for young ladies, something that I didn't liked so much, since I also came from a girls High School. The only men I lived with were my father & 2 brothers and had friends, who were more men than women.

At the same time I studied piano with a private teacher, whom I loved very much because he taught me to see a beautiful world through music, he was a great pianist and teacher, he used to say he was my spiritual father and I could feel his love. I met him when I was 10 years old, my mother had taken me with another teacher, but Mr. Arceo was her friend since youth and now he was a piano teacher. His complete name was José Arceo Jácome, I owe him to have learned how to share music with others as food for their soul and my own. He taught me how to transport myself with melodies to beautiful and enchanted places. With him I not only acquired the technique and interpretation of it, but also the freedom to express and passionately feel the music.

This love for music is what has led me to investigate more about the feelings and emotions of others. Music as food of the soul, as the support in moments of sadness, as encouragement to achieve goals, music as the expression of the most beautiful in art and the expression of oneself.

Mother also took me to ballet lessons and for me it was and still today is a joy to dance and enjoy my body.

I always had private piano lessons and at the age of 24 I signed up for the National Conservatory of Music in Mexico City, I wanted to obtain the title of Professional Musician and he encouraged me to do so I remember that he told me: you will need official papers to help yourself in what you will build in the future because you are a teacher at heart.

I had to take the 1st grade of several subjects, no matter if my level was 8th of the pianist career. I did it and I was very bored in some subjects because I felt very slow and unsustainable teaching, I knew more theory because I already was already a performer, I interpreted music of great composers as Debussy, Beethoven, Mussorgsky, Khachaturian, Prokofieff, Bartók, Liszt, etc. it was a difficult time, but I could not 'jump' those mandatory steps in the school. I only spent 2 years there since my responsibilities as a mother of 2 children demanded my attention and we also moved abroad.

But the papers I achieved during those years at the Conservatory of Music, helped me to prove that I had knowledge of music when I opened my Music School in 1989 in the City of Querétaro. Maestro Arceo no longer saw that, he died on February 22, 1986.

I always wanted to be a musician!

In my house music was always present. When I expressed my desire to go to the Conservatory, I would be about 17 years old, my mother said no, because it was a place for hippies. At that time not so much freedom of expression was allowed because they were considered acts of rebellion towards parents. Anyway, I was a rebel! (according to my mother).

I was very sad for not being able to go to the Conservatory. Then I decided that I would go to High School and then to the University since I was also attracted to study Biology and Chemistry.

There again I experienced another disappointment. My mother said that I could not go to University because it was more important for my brothers to study a career than me, because at the end they would support a family and I would get married in the future. I cried, cried and cried.

I was enrolled in the best school for secretaries and I always got the 1st. place in the 4 years I attended there. I graduated as the best student of my generation with Honors. These studies have also helped me a lot in the development of my dream that was to have my own Music School. I started with that idea since 1981.

In 1986, I met a piano teacher who had a young daughter with cerebral palsy and visited me to ask me to sing some songs that she had composed to help her daughter improve her gross and fine motor coordination. That caught my attention a lot, I already had in my blood, as I said before, the spirit of a 'rescuer'.

I learned a lot with that teacher, whose name is Margarita Velázquez, I learned from her dedication, her passion, her generosity, she worked for APAC (Association for Pro Cerebral Paralysis) and hence the desire was born in me to compose songs for children to help them in their knowledge of body parts, improve fine and gross coordination, spatial awareness, language, articulation, as well to make it easier for them to understand music theory in a pleasant way with funny songs. My idea was that children could learn about music in a more joyful way and not as boring as in the Conservatory of Music as in those days.

It was then for the year of 1987 in the month of February, that I copyrighted my program of Music for Babies and Children 'AYRAM'®

Finally, my family and I moved to the city of Querétaro, Mexico in 1989 and there I built the First School for Babies and Children "Titi- tá ". With great success during the years it worked.

In 1993 I started with classes for pregnant women that came once a week for prenatal stimulation. I continued composing songs and fairytales with music that carried a message of motivation to achieve goals in life and appreciate beauty, which I also recorded in cassettes (at that time) and were part of the educational material of the children who attended my school along with a series of Solfeggio workbooks, based on the Kódaly method, in which, based on syllables, music was measured and greatly helped the acquisition of articulation in language and thinking processes.

From 1998 to 2007 I traveled to different parts of the world being a lecturer about my Music program. On the first trip, July 1998, I presented my Music Program to the ISME (International Society of Music Education) in Stellensbosch , at the Seminar organized by Dr. Sheila Woodward and at the International Congress in Pretoria in South Africa; and it was there in Pretoria that I met a music professional who, with knowledge of psychology, helped the mothers of babies to connect with them after having been through traumatic moments at birth and from there my interest in knowing more about the subject.

I returned to Mexico and at my desk I found a booklet that said: Congress at the University of St. Mary in London, England, the theme " Consciousness of Birth ", this was like a magnet for me! I would say, it was calling me, timing was just perfect.

The incredible thing is that it was held one month after I arrived from South Africa, and then I decided to request financial support again from another government institution. For travelling to South Africa I was sponsored by the Secretary of Education of the State of Querétaro, in those days directed by Dr. Gabriel Siade Barquet, a very sensitive man dedicated to the improvement of education.

The support for England was given to me by CONCYTEQ (Council of Science and Technology of the State of Querétaro) at that time, directed by Mr. Alejandro Alfredo Lozano Guzmán.

These two incredible sponsors allowed me to see beyond the doors of my school into the world of congresses of Music and Psychology, I was invited to participate in several cities of the United States, either with my music program or with musical participations with our folkloric group, performing Mexican music that was being taught at my school, cities like Washington DC, Seattle, Vancouver; Phoenix, Arizona; San Francisco California; Williamsburg, Virginia; St. Paul, Minneapolis; We also had the opportunity to go to Merida, Venezuela in July 1999 to participate in the 2nd. Latin Congress of the ISME with the children's folkloric orchestra of the school directed by Mtro. Jorge Alberto Jara de León, LEM whom at present still conducts the Tonalli Typical Orchestra with great success, more than 24 years after starting his activities at this school.

I also presented my work on Auditory Discrimination in Babies of One Year of Age, for the Congress of Music of Asian Countries at the University of Launceston , Tasmania, in February 2000, a wonderful trip that allowed me to meet amazing people and to enjoy a Mozart's opera at the wonderful Sydney Opera House, Australia.

At the presentation in San Francisco, Calif . I met Dr. Joann O'Leary, Member of the APPPAH (Association for Prenatal and Perinatal Psychology and Health) Master in Psychology from the University of Belfast and a

Masters in Maternal and Child Health from the University of Minnesota, who presented a study on The Meaning of Paternity after the Loss of a Baby, she invited me in April 1999 to Minnesota to present my prenatal stimulation work with pregnant women and conduct a workshop with nurses who attended high-risk and single pregnant teenagers . I returned to Minnesota in April 2000, I met several prenatal psychologists and from there they invited me to my first conference in Europe, this was for the ISPPM Congress of Medicine (International Society for Prenatal Psychology and Medicine) the subject: Diseases Psychosomatic during pregnancy, this congress took place on the Island of Sardinia in Italy in June 2000.

By the end of that year I moved to England and being there I had the opportunity to learn about Personality Analysis and Auras Reading with Vivian John Crowhurst in 2001, we both studied Prenatal Psychology with Dr. JonRG Turner and his wife TroyaGN Turner, pioneers in the field, in May 2002 in the city of Tilburg , NL. That same year on the following month I was invited as one of the 5 special guests at the University of Ivanovo, Russia, to present my work and sign in the University's Book of Distinguished Visitors.

A new world of possibilities and knowledge ahead for me to learn more about the impact of our prenatal memories in our lives.

I had always been a woman that pursues what I want, giving my best and making myself present and making people feel good, either with my music or with my company.

Why do I tell you all this?

Because I also remember my prenatal history. I was not conscious of it, as it has happened to many of us, but when I was trained as a Prenatal Psychologist in 2002.

I became aware of all what had happened at my birth! I was living now in England and had the opportunity to attend to a Course on Prenatal Psychology, to which I had been invited 4 years earlier by the **Psic. Jon RG Turner**, he knew my music work with pregnant women and mothers & babies and told me that as soon as I could to take that course because it would open other horizons of understanding for the work I was doing.

It was at the Congress of Birth with Consciousness, in September 1998, in the City of London, England at the University of Saint Mary, that I learned about Prenatal Psychology, great pioneers, great teachers: **Michael Odent , Jon RG Turner, David Chamberlain, William Emerson, Ludwig Janus , Grigori Breckman , Thomas Verny** , to mention a few; and then I saw the importance of being aware of the emotions of pregnant women through music. Listening to his teachings was like that honey that sweetened my ears.

I had a lot to learn!

I decided not to go unnoticed, so I was in high school and was the best student, with the highest average. I was part of the escort for the Mexican flag every week during high school, I spoke at important ceremonies. Looking back I discovered in the Prenatal Memories course that when someone tells me: 'you can't or it is not your turn, you don't understand, don't think about that, I asked you to shut up, what are you doing here ?, who asked for your opinion? ' and phrases like those, took me back to the moment when the doctor denied my presence in the womb. My mother has always had great faith in the doctors and blindly believes everything they say, therefore, she accepted what this doctor told her and became sad.

I always like to question the reason for what it is said with such authority. I do research on my own, draw conclusions.

My parents went to see another doctor soon after because my mother felt ill and the surprise was that he confirmed she was pregnant! I was, without any intention from my mom, ignored for about 3 months, but after that, she just wanted me so much. Despite this, my mother was worried thinking that she could lose me too, since before getting pregnant with me, she had two other pregnancies and they were lost in the first trimester each. I was natural birth and on the time expected at home. I was received by the doctor and my maternal grandmother. The first thing my grandmother (Mama Tita) said was: what a beautiful girl! They received me with joy.

I still have a letter that my father wrote to me when I turned fifteen years old and in which he mentioned the day I was born; I will share it with you:

> MARIA, *my dear daughter:*

> *Today that you go through the golden doors of illusion,*

always remember this moment as a landscape that appears before your eyes full of light and color.

Beautiful will be the day, where you'll hear the sweet trilling of love finches, the path that you will walk will be covered with beautiful flowers with a soft scent and you will dream and contemplate infinite skies studded with white stars.

You, my little one,
that in the mystical hour of a calm sunset,
You came like a shining light by our side
You have filled our lives with rich blessings
and beautiful joys.
You came to us at that time
and it was his Divine Will
that you will occupy the place of virtue.

We have laughed in your sweet childhood, we have enjoyed in your adolescence and now, my sweet girl, my supreme love, go through life with a firm step, always leading being ahead: for the poor your tender affection, for the rich your understanding, for the children your human love, for the elderly sweet attention, your friends sincere affection, for the enemy peace and forgiveness; for your brothers eternal love, for your parents veneration and to the Eternal God who in this life gives us tenderness, always offers your very life, your thoughts and your heart.

Maybe there comes a time when you stumble upon a rock, when the cruel sting hurts you, maybe there will be a night when your crying becomes bitter because of a sad disappointment, you may not find light to guide you for a moment, but remember, always remember my sweet girl, that there in heaven, God is very loving and do not take your eyes away from him and here on earth there is a nest where your parents like doves, always the wings will extend to cover you from the storms, to protect you from the evils and to give you soft heat.

Your dad.
March 8, 1967.

I can state that I had the most beautiful of the receptions when I was born.

This contributed to the fact that the prenatal memory of being ignored was healed by the way I was born, the place and who I was surrounded with so much love.

Some years ago, I remember describing to my mother the room I was born in, the bed, the curtains, the color, who was there, the door of the room. She was surprised and confirmed the details, but she didn't tell me more. I even remember the smile of my Mom Tita (my grandmother) and her hands holding me. That is all I remember.

I had a happy childhood in general, I was always a dreamer person therefore somehow 'created my worlds'. I was very close with my maternal grandmother until she died in an accident after falling from a passenger truck when she descended from it, I was 7 years old and I remember her singing voice, her constant smile, she was so beautiful! I started piano lessons at age 5, I loved music from the beginning. My mom played the piano and accompanied my Mom Tita when she sang.

What I discovered about myself when I studied Prenatal Psychology was that much of what I do today I bring in my emotional DNA and reinforced it in my childhood. My passion is music and work with pregnant women and their babies.

My mother had 11 pregnancies, only 4 of us were born. Perhaps seeing her pregnant and then losing the babies led me to think that pregnant women were fragile and had to be taken care of. I only remember when I was 10 years old that I cried a lot when I knew that the baby my mother was expecting had died, I saw how my mother cried since she came into our apartment and went to her bedroom to her bed and cried.

My pain was very etched. When she was pregnant last time, they had to do a cervical cerclage, the treatment consists of a strong suture inserted in and around the cervix in the early stage of pregnancy, this so that an abortion does not occur, let's say so that the baby stays safe in the womb. This is how my sister was gestated, she was received with great pleasure from us the 3 siblings. I wanted to have a sister so much and I was very happy when she was born. My mother did not get pregnant again, she was risking her life every time

When I got married, I was educated in psycho-prophylactic delivery. In the year of 1973 the Lamaze method for natural birth began to be accepted. My gynecologist and his wife were among the first to work that way in Mexico City.

My two children were born by natural birth, without epidural, full term and healthy. There was only one difference in their emotional aspect. My first pregnancy was beautiful, quiet, in a very clean city without pollution, without stress, I slept a couple of naps a day of 2 hours each. I played the piano every day, sang and sang to my baby. I went to my Lamaze classes and when the child was born, everything went well and without problems.

My second pregnancy ran the same way in the same city, I also slept the 2 naps of 2 hours each. My first child did not give me a problem as to his sleeping time, he was a very calm and smiling baby. We slept together.

The difference between my second pregnancy and the first one was that when I was 2 months pregnant, I went to the market, in front of the building where we lived, to bring some flowers and oranges. To go faster, I left my 1-year-old baby in the crib, asleep, and took the dog with me. I went to do the shopping and came back in 20 minutes A child came to help me to carry my bag of oranges and when I arrived at the building, I opened the front door and a man on a bicycle came out, I did not recognize him as a worker there. The building had an intercom system to open to anyone who requested it as long as the person was identified.

The dog was barking at the man who was leaving, but I didn't think in that moment it was important. We went upstairs to the 2nd. floor where I lived. When I removed my key to open my door, I realize that it was opened and paired. I got a big surprise when I opened the door, everything was in disarray, drawers of the dresser in the living room, turned around, all the clothes scattered on the floor and I saw my jewelry boxes open and empty, they had robbed me!

My heart skipped a beat thinking of my baby who was in the crib. The distance from the entrance door to the door of my son's bedroom (about 3 meters) became eternal. The adrenaline rush must have been such that my body was shaking.

The boy who accompanied me put the bags on the floor of the room and waited to see what happened. I arrived at my baby's room and there he was, sitting in the crib, sucking his finger (he did not use to suck it, from that day and on till his 3 yrs old he sucked it) now I know it was anguish, seeing the stranger and hearing all the noise he made, maybe he got scared. Now that I remember the incident, I ask myself: could it had been that the man yelled at him? Maybe he scared him by making some ugly face. Was he aware of the baby in his crib? I will not know that.

I took him out of the crib, hugged him and ran down to the little store in the corner to ask permission to call my husband from their phone.

Already a neighbor was with me, the owner of the store reassured me, I just hugged the baby tightly and cried inconsolably, I never remembered that I was pregnant, I did not tell my daughter to be born what was happening, I did not comfort her, nor I rubbed my belly, I simply forgot about it.

When my husband arrived with his boss, I remember well, that he carried the child and told me: 'Calm down, you both are fine, remember you're pregnant.'

That's when I became aware of my unborn baby!

That was the traumatic event my daughter suffered. Shee was born healthy, not very big, small, full term. Natural delivery without epidural, very fast and with very strong contractions. For a moment I felt out of breath and I said: "I can't, I can't." Her dad told me: 'Of course you can, we are almost there'. She was born quickly, in the 2nd. push and all good.

Unlike my first pregnancy, she did have a moment of anguish with the event of theft. Two different births in spite of taking care of my environment. The boy took 12 hours of labor, but in the calmest way. The girl took 4 and a half hours in total since the labor began and the contractions were stronger.

The two have different responses to difficult times. My son takes them easy and with a little bit more control. My daughter gets nervous, accelerates and sometimes loses control. Each one has worked on their holistic development in the way that has favored them the most. As adults they are excellent and good parents.

What has made me proud is the way my daughter lived her last childbirth, the third, with much more awareness on how to bring a baby into the world, in an environment full of love and enthusiasm, with a wonderful husband and so eager of having a child, that birth was in water and at home!

I support waterbirth at home although I know it is important to always consider the circumstances around. When my children were born, I didn't know about the possibility of having a waterbirth. They were practically born at home, because Dr. Canales, the gynecologist who treated me, had enabled his home as a hospital. There were only 3 rooms (what were bedrooms) one was the delivery room and the other two for the patients to stay and recover. When my children were born there was no one else in the place, only us as a family. I thought that was fantastic! There was stillness, no loud corridors, no regrets in adjoining rooms or sirens, none of that.

The stay of each of my children in that hospital was two days; Both were born on Thursday and we left on Saturday to travel from Mexico City to the City of Toluca, where we lived.

CHAPTER X: THERE ARE MORE CASES OF REAL LIFE

XANDRA y CESARE - 48 y 49 years old

This couple came to therapy because their relationship was getting worse and with 20 years of marriage they were in a dead end. Xandra was determined to divorce and Cesare still wanted to keep hope of continuing the marriage.

A week before I did a personality analysis of his two male children of 20 and 19 years old, who showed that both needed more parental presence and to feel acknowledge by both parents, they expressed they were tired of the daily conflicts and fights at home, without them being able to make a decision about their parents' problems.

Within their analysis the boys were depressed. the eldest was confused because he did not understood what was happening between his parents, although he severely judged the father because he felt he was being manipulated and that made him sad, he felt rejected and was angry at himself, and his mother confused him as well because she really gave him a double message and he preferred to evade her by putting distance between her and him.

The youngest son also felt manipulated and had little appreciation for the father, said that the discussions at home already had him tired and his feeling was to shout loudly, explode and ask his mother to shut up, he felt that they ignored him and that both parents worked too much, it would be best to put an end to this, and most of all he wanted to feel like a real man. Somehow both boys felt that they did not have a male role model that was emotional balanced and loving, and their self-esteem was very low. Both boys were born by caesarean section.

Therefore, I called the parents to com to a therapy session to find out how they could help their children and to talk about how much damage was done to their relationship.

Xandra said she was tired of how things were happening since a few years ago. She is a strong woman with many guarded resentments, and he has a belief that he must work hard to deserve love and reward.

When I started the analysis, the first thing I saw was that they both no longer wanted guidance, but to express what they were feeling and above all she blamed him a lot for what happened, he also complained and said that he had missed setting limits because she was extremely manipulative.

The result of the analysis was that Cesare, the firstborn, had a very strong birth trauma because he was not planned and his mother had tried to abort him, but in the end she continued with her husband and Cesare's father abandoned them when he was 11 years old, therefore, had no role model in his teens and grew up without knowing how to make decisions and with a very low self-esteem. Seeing how his mother worked too hard to support 4 young children, his behavior hardened, she did not know how to give them tenderness and there was no time for that. Currently, he has spoken with his mother already understanding the situation and his mother apologized one day for not knowing how to love them as they deserved.

In the case of Xandra , she was the firstborn, and with a mother who did not appreciated herself and made frequent excuses to the husband when he wanted to go for a walk with her, he got tired and gave up inviting her, and at some point he had an affair with another woman. For Xandra that meant that his father would not make the least effort to conquer her mother's love, so when her mother discovered his affair, she argued with him, this happened when Xandra was 13 years old. His father was her hero and he failed to her.

She says she loved her father so much and caused her a lot of confusion all this and now she understood and forgave him, to which I replied that it is about understanding not forgiving. She has the belief that men fail, that they are useless, and they don't know how to make decisions on time; this belief is confirmed by seeing that Cesare loses good job opportunities for not making decisions on time.

The analysis also showed that Xandra in her childhood was sexually abused by a close relative and she had not told anyone, neither her husband knew it. She grew up in fear of intimacy and there are also failures within the couple. Cesare said that it was the first time he had knowledge of that, Xandra say that she had been sexually abused, for him it was a surprise and he began to understand many things.

Xandra blames him for lack of attention for her and her children for always working and she takes refuge at work. Neither of them is doing what brings them passion. They have made the decision to make changes regarding this issue.

I explained to them the negative picture of what will happen due to their dysfunctions, in case they would get divorced; I also explained the positive outcome if they wished to continue. They decided to continue receiving professional advice for couples and thus rescue their marriage and their family. Cesare is the one who is most willing to do this. It is very understandable for what Xandra has lived throughout her life.

Once again it is confirmed how the subconscious chooses another person with equal dysfunctions in a matter of prenatal memory to rescue and prove themselves that rejection, abandonment is there for them to happen.

NEHA - 30 years old

Neha's story is fascinating. Neha was adopted 16 days after birth. She feels that she is not taken seriously in her feelings and always feels used, as if she is an object. It happens with relatives as well with other people around her.

Neha was born from a couple who already had a child. Neha's biological father is the nephew of her adoptive father. Neha's biological mother is about 25 years old when she conceived her. Within this family there are hierarchies. They are a family of ancestry and with good economic position.

Why is Neha adopted if she is born in an already established family?

It happens that his biological father's uncle's wife cannot conceive. They have the belief that a curse has been imposed on the family because one of the great-great-grandfathers exploited and enslaved a woman and she cursed him that he would not count on offspring, this woman could not defend herself from the power of this man.

Her biological father is the only surviving male of several who were born and then died. Then the aunt who couldn't have children asked Neha's biological mother that, if she gave birth to a girl, to give her to her and that she would raise her as a mother. At first, they were surprised by the request, but after Neha was born the mother hesitated to give the child away.

But Neha's father loved and respected his uncle and they agreed to give the baby to him and his wife, anyway he was not a man who expressed affection so easily. When Neha was born, the aunt reminded to her niece about her promise and on the 16th day of Neha's birth, she was handed over to the aunt who had wanted so much to become a mother. The aunt and the niece loved each other very much and ignored 'unknowingly' Neha's feelings for the desire to please the aunt by giving her a daughter.

Neha's biological parents already had a son, Neha was the second daughter, after her a boy and a girl arrived. These 3 brothers grew up with their biological parents.

Neha has trouble establishing relationships with women. When analyzing the way in which she was treated from her prenatal life, it is not strange that she cannot trust women. Her mother did not completely bond with her because she had already made a promise to give her up for adoption.

She says that she somehow understands the arrangement between her relatives, but it always happens to her that, if people tend to decide for her or ignore her comments, she gets very upset. She comments that she also feels relegated when the two women (their mothers) are together enjoying time and do not include her. They have a very special connection. She has expressed her feelings to them, but still she has not felt loved by any of them.

Seems to her that her biological mother had no remorse about giving her away. When Neha is born, she doubts a bit, but in the end after 16 days of birth she gave her child to her aunt. Here what happens in the girl is the feeling of a huge lack of power, which translates into a lack of confidence in herself and others. The feeling that you have the power to make decisions is something very important in life, because it helps us to achieve what we want.

The adoptive mother did not carried her in her womb, she only wanted her as a companion object, rather the adoptive mother wanted her to feel herself like a mother without thinking about what the baby really needed, and the best could had been her biological mother.

A situation of selfishness that Neha now confronts. Not only with their mothers, but with those around her. She is very sensitive to lack of empathy and understanding. And what bothers her the most is to realize that men have only seen her as an object of pleasure. She doesn't know how to get out of these manipulation traps that she falls into many times. Knowing subconsciously that they can 'control you' makes her, in some way, feel comfortable in a relationship until she realizes that it is a toxic relationship and that what she wants is to get out of it. The relationship ends and the feeling of abandonment, helplessness and anger comes.

She is learning to separate from toxic people, now she realizes, knowing where her sense of rejection comes from, that she can put an end to certain relationships on which she becomes dependent.

Unfortunately, she gets into conflict with herself, thinking that she should not withdraw from the people who 'take care' of her. Many times, this kind of 'care' is a subtle manipulation, Neha is 'used' to be treated like this.

She is familiar with the verbal and body language that hooks her to live under toxic relationships, it's like needing them to feel good. By being aware of the way she interprets them, she makes more intelligent and courageous decisions.

SILVIO - 18 years old

Silvio wonders why he should stay virgin to marriage if there are many women who do not arrive virgin to it, although he wishes to have a woman who has never been touched by anyone else and could only be first for him. After a therapy done with Cognitive Image Profiling, he realizes that he carries a lot of masculine information of manipulation, control, machismo and disdain towards the women; then he questions himself about being caring and loving. On the other hand, he comes from a family of divorced parents, when he was very young, 6 years old, his father left home for another woman. Surprisingly for the family, the father does not recognize a sensible boy in Silvio and advises him to do atrocities such as sexually abusing women, the exact words of the father are: 'well, take the one you want!'

When Silvio understands the importance of becoming pregnant and what the baby can receive then confirms that his desire is to have a wife who has not been touched by anyone, who is a virgin. In this world today it might seem crazy because sexual activity is taken so lightly. Although many times it is not given the sacred and spiritual value it has. Here the important thing to rescue is that noble and loving personality in Silvio, for himself and for women; he knows that the baby will receive all the emotions from the mother, mainly, and from him as a father by contributing to the emotions of the mother.

If a girl becomes pregnant out of wedlock, she begins to feel guilt, frustration, loneliness, fear, anguish, anger, and in many circumstances, she wants to abort the baby. In some cases, women, either by themselves, carry it out or at the request of the partner. Wanting to get rid of the baby, no love and such negative feelings and emotions do not contribute to human beings being emotionally healthy.

MENA - 25 years old

She is a young woman who does not understand why every time someone talks to her about love, she immediately becomes distressed and even has depression. She ended the relationship with her boyfriend 24 years old, since she felt that at any moment, he could leave her.

The boy was a very responsible and committed person, he could not understand why Mena acted as if he was going to cheat on her, or to suddenly disappear from her life, etc.

Mena's fear was such that her boyfriend began to feel that perhaps he was not good enough for her. The relationship deteriorated and in a few months it dissolved.

Mena is a lovely, smart and overprotective girl, but when it comes to relating more intimately with people, she goes into depression.

Speaking about her birth, apparently throughout the pregnancy her mother suffered from depression because her father was not at home, since he worked away from home and only went to visit during weekends. Although she shared time with her mother (or Mena's grandmother), she was a woman who did not value herself, she was very dependent on the husband and when he had to go to work outside the city, she became depressed.

Mena's birth was a natural birth, but with a heartless mother. Mena was born in The Netherlands.

A few months after Mena was born, the mother became pregnant again with her sister and because she was still depressed, Mena, being still an 8-month-old baby, was sent to her uncles' house in England to be raised by him.

Can you imagine what that baby felt when she was uprooted from her father's house, her land and her customs at such an early age? Besides that, without any explanation!

The uncles raised her and gave her a good home. Even so, Mena felt a void in her heart. It was as if the joy of living was gone. What we have to remember is that we have been gestating in our mother's womb and for the first 9 months of life we are still a unity with our mothers, being ripped off before the natural separation begins causes anxiety and confusion in us.

In spite of understanding that the separation with her mother in some way was traumatic for her, because she was not in control, had no power of decision, it had left an invisible and painful impact in his mind and heart. She had the wrong belief that anyone she loved would end up leaving her at any time. That uncertainty somehow is present through daily behavior until it becomes a behavior accepted by the individual, it becomes a limiting belief.

Somehow the last two relationships she had only lasted about 7 months each. Curiously close to the time she lived in the paternal house before being sent to the uncle's house. Mena will have to work in therapy that belief that she is not important and can be treated as an object.

KARLA - 34 years old

Karla finds it difficult to relate because she somehow chooses people who are usually in constant motion.

She is born in a family of artists. Her parents are very busy people and she is in the care of her babysitter. She was not breastfed because the mother did not want to, her activities did not allow her to take care of the baby in that way, therefore, she was given formula. It is not bad that she had to take the formula, it is food. Even if the mother had not breastfed her, if the mother herself had given her the bottle with milk, that would have somehow helped Karla to believe that she can be loved without being set aside because she was not a priority in her mother's life.

There are studies that reveal the fact that being breastfed stimulates the love hormone in mother and baby. Both looking at each other, completes a circle of mother / child dialogue that allows both to be able to feel and express love, compassion, empathy, etc. How I am fed and the reaction I have to the fact of being fed and the person who feeds me establishes my reaction for life to allow me to receive food, energy, money and any kind of support.

If the food has an emotional value - pleasure, love, comfort, satisfaction - there may be a challenge to protect myself of being overweight in my life. If I hate food or I am being forced to take it as a newborn, at some point in my life I can develop eating disorders such as anorexia or bulimia nervosa, even serious addictions.

Karla accepts to be helped in complicated situations but often simply shuts up and tries to get things sorted out by herself. This is very common in people who either were not breastfed or who another person, who was not their mother, did.

ESTEFANIA - 31 years old

She is 31 years old and has had several love disappointments. Little by little she is feeling sad and less worthy as a woman. Apparently, she grew up in a loving environment, which I began to doubt when I saw his love failures. She has been hanging out with a guy 34 years old. Well educated man whom a year ago initiated a friendship with her and now is wanting to take the relationship farther to an engagement.

Estefanía puts up barriers and annoys herself, because she is romantically attracted to him and has a hard time letting him get closer. When we made an analysis of his personality and told her that I saw that there had been problems in his mother's pregnancy, she was very surprised because she didn't want to mention anything about that because apparently it did not matter.

It turns out she had been a twin. Her twin died within the first trimester of pregnancy, apparently it was a natural loss, there was no surgery, the baby left the womb naturally. Therefore, Estefanía was left 'alone'. When this happened, that feeling of loneliness and loss remained in the unconsciousness of the unborn baby and she carried it throughout her life without knowing where was coming from.

An anxiety and fear of 'dying' of being 'abandoned' is created in her mind. Then, in adulthood, when it comes to establishing a serious love relationship, she do not commit herself because of fear, and ignores the intentions of the other person because she believes in her subconscious that he will not love her forever and that he could leave her.

She tells me that she has gone with several holistic therapists and they have not been able to get her out of her anxiety state, until now she understands where it comes from and already knows how to deal with it. Of course, there are many exercises to be done to collapse those wrong beliefs that were created along with it.

Understanding that it is not men who abandon her, but that she 'pushes' them out of her life, she begins to make the necessary changes and accepts that her perception of men was not the truth of her reality.

She has spent part of her life looking for her soulmate and has not been able to find satisfaction with anyone, in general she has trouble trusting others.

While the source of love (the mother) was sad and anxious, she did not know that the baby had to be explained about that loss when she was born and assured her the love they felt for her and the desire for her to be born healthy.

Those emotions belonged to the mother and permeated Estefania's subconscious and believed them as her own. This prevented her from opening with confidence to a love relationship.

She has understood the source of the problem and will take the necessary measures to establish the relationship with this boy with confidence and without fear of being abandoned. There are several ways to help her nowadays.

CHAPTER XI: NEONATO DURING THE WORLD WAR II!

Let's talk about this case since it is somewhat complicated due to the damage caused, involuntarily to this human being.

Vivian John Crowhurst was born on June 29, 1944 in Rugby, England, days after Day D, historically, the term **D-day** is used to refer to June 6, 1944 in **World War II** , the day it began to run the so-called Operation Overlord , battle in Normandy, France to stop the German armed forces. Operation that ended on August 25, 1944.

John is currently 75 years old. He is an exceptional painter! From a very young age he was listed as retarded at school because he spent time in contemplation and the only thing that was happening is that he dreamed awake. It goes without saying that he was one of those children isolated and rejected by his classmates and teachers to the extent of even telling him that he was not fit to learn.

Within that early childhood he was subjected to abuse from his classmates, for some time he was in a boarding school and apparently witnessed sexual abuse by teachers towards some of his classmates, he says he used to hide in the bathrooms; sometimes I wonder if it really was just his teammates or if it happened to him or was about to happen to him.

I mention this because in his adult life he is distressed and even gets angry just knowing that this is happening to children, like what is heard in the news about pedophiles in many parts of the world.

Although the subject anguishes and annoys him, he still feeds on listening this kind of news. It is like an addiction.

Vivian John was sent to a school for children with disabilities so he could learn at his own pace. With this the belief of being a child good for nothing, the belief was emphasized.

His parents were not the most loving people in the world; his father, a mechanical engineer during the war, he built the turbines for the jets. Somehow his father focused on his work and every afternoon he built scale aircraft. John was fascinated by his work, but his father did not allow him to touch anything or help him build his planes, therefore, again the rejection is what Vivian John received.

His mother was a sick woman, she had a heart murmur that did not allow her to lead a normal active life. In fact, Vivian John comments that during the years after the war, till his 6 years old, he had not tried orange juice, since his mother was the one who had to drink it due to her constant physical weakness.

It was until after his sixth anniversary and that the economic and social situation improved in his country, that he could be fed better. He uses a very common phrase: 'I can live only by eating potatoes, bread and tea'.

It is impressive how this man with the talent he has for painting and writing has not been able to completely heal these memories of being rejected, feeling like a loser, a failure and has become self-destructive.

Here we can notice that an individual, not for being bright and intelligent in his profession, necessarily has Emotional Intelligence. You can achieve a balance in life, the changes are made by the person when there is true commitment for a better life

Through his personal therapy sessions, he has made changes in his behaviors, but he mentions that the demons of the past continue to torment him, and he is overwhelmed.

A common denominator in the healing of the soul in a human being, has to do on how much faith the person has in the Divinity and in the talents that have been granted.

Something that marked Vivian John in his intrauterine life was the fact that his maternal grandfather died in the attack to The Hood, supposedly the best English black ship, in which he was serving as a soldier, by the Bismarck, a better German ship.. This traumatic event for the mother in gestation permeated to the unborn baby, imagine the mother's adrenaline rush to the baby! Of course, without intention.

After that, the mother also began to live with anxiety because she was a descendant of Jews, although she did not profess that religion. At that time Hitler had ordered that even all those people with a Jewish last name should be brought to the concentration camps. They never found her, but the mere threat of being caught also affected the unborn baby.

It is therefore understood the defensive behavior of Vivian John that intensifies with the experiences of a painful divorce after 17 years of marriage. He is abandoned by his wife and children. At that time, the year of 1985, he worked for an editorial in Johannesburg, South Africa.

For 5 years they lived there, his wife did not end up adapting to the culture and returned to England, leaving him alone. Vivian John continued with his art making beautiful paintings of birds of prey, which had to be left in South Africa at his brother's house since he could not take them back due to the high cost of transportation.

Vivian John returns to England to wanting to make an agreement with his wife May and he achieves nothing, then gives the house to his wife and children, jobless and falls into depression to the extent of trying to commit suicide. His son passed by his house that day to greet him and found him in very bad condition, he was taken to the hospital where he recovered. Again, he began again with his art, now with pencil drawing, making portraits, he has always been fascinated to draw people and their emotions.

Feeling rejected and a failure, he emigrated to Australia where he was expected by a woman (Margaret) who had met him in South Africa when his wife had abandoned him, and argued that the son he had was his, he never checked on that and in his desire to have a family he agreed to go to that country and start over.

But their relationship lasted 6 months because the woman was addicted to drugs and had a relationship with another man. She let him know about this affair and asked for his deportation. Again, rejected and unsuccessful returns to England.

He remained single for 16 years, was related to women who somehow 'used' him, and he still was unsuccessful. He continued with his art and prepared as a therapist in Oxford, England. He took courses in Outlook Training, directed by Jane Duncan, psychotherapist, and author of several books including "Change your Thoughts , Change your Life " and Philip Rogers, her husband trained in turn , by Louise Hay that at that time they owned a Health Clinic in that city and basing his workshops in the principles of Louise Hay's Therapy.

Louise Hay, American writer and speaker considered one of the most representative figures of the New Thought movement and precursor of self-help books (October 8, 1926 - August 30, 2017)

This knowledge about self finally started to help him. Still he had not been successful in a loving relationship.

Having studied and participated for 10 years in self-improvement workshops, he created the wonderful CIP personality analysis system, Cognitive Imaging Profiling ® (Cognitive Profile) based on images and symbols that reveal the subconscious information.

System that has become the main tool of my work, for therapeutic help in individuals with emotional blockages since the prenatal phase, in my daily practice for 19 years.

In June of the year 2000 he met who until now is his wife. He improved in his art, refined his therapeutic work towards other people, he has made interesting changes, but his demons are still stalking him. In 2002 he received a rebirth therapy that made him understand his intrauterine life. He prepared himself as a Prenatal Therapist with JonRG Turner and TroyaGN Turner, directors of the Whole Self Institute in the Netherlands.

Both the PAM, Prebirth Awakening Matrix (Awakening of Prenatal Memories) and the CIP (Cognitive Profile) are very valuable therapies for the emotional healing in people, since the first consultation it defines the situation that hinders the emotional well-being of the individual.

I wanted to comment on Vivian John's case so people can realize how terrible it can be to grow in a toxic uterus. Not only people who have been born during the war have this disability; what about drug addicted mothers, alcoholics, abused women by their partner physically and verbally, poverty, disease, unconsciousness, ignorance, loneliness, fear, single mothers, abandoned mothers, what is behind all that?

CHAPTER XII: PRENATAL LIFE AND BIRTH

MIRACLES TO CARE!

AWARENESS

It is very important that pregnant women become aware of the importance of gestating a baby. There is much happiness around on many occasions and there is sadness and frustration on others, when a woman decides to get pregnant she has to be aware of the importance of gestating a New Life in her womb, the center of her power as a woman, the sanctuary where she is nourishing a human life.

There is a lot to talk about the responsibility of women, but as well when a man decides to be intimate with a woman must also be aware of the repercussions of his participation in this sacred act of intercourse.

When a couple decides to conceive a baby, each moment of intimacy should be full of happiness, desire, love, both towards themselves and towards the other and of course to the baby to conceive.

When a couple is only intimate by mere carnal desire without taking any precaution not to conceive, there is no respect for themselves or the other and less for a possible baby.

Within the psychology of prenatal therapy there is much talk about this sacred moment as the basis for a being to feel completely loved, expected, longed for and desired.

Starting with this kind of attitude, parents become even more aware of the responsibility that they are acquiring and how that seed of love that they will take care of, will live on fertile soil.

Let us be aware of how damaged society is because there have been many violations against women, imposition and control, decrease in their gender, restriction and in many parts of the world including the complete nullification of their rights. We know that in all countries there is abuse towards women, that is why there is so much dysfunction in the world, not because we know of some places where women are mistreated, means that is not happening in millions of homes, it is not being known by the public in other places, that is all! but it does exist abuse towards women and a denial of their importance within the family and society.

The woman is the **Source of Life and the Source of Love** and she has to start by rescuing that inner strength and that value, that gift that was given to her to procreate, a woman has to love her body, to value it; if she becomes blessed with children, her body will be the sanctuary where they will live for about 9 months, where a new human being is created, the outer world will be seen by the baby as the **world he lived in the womb**.

Then let's think about this:

- What kind of society do we want?
- How do we want to see this transformed world?
- How do we want to live?
- What quality of life will we offer to the children we will gestate?
- How much more are we willing to tolerate in terms of abuse towards women?
- What does it need to happen for us to react in favor to respect women?

Let's take care of women all of us; women and men, let's take care of them since they are girls, babies, since their life in the womb. Let us recognize that from the womb of these women humans, both men and women, will be procreated.

The greatest blessing that a baby can have is to have a healthy mother, holistically speaking, a mother who can be dedicated to her children without worries to survive, knowing she is protected by a man who loves her, who respects her and whose desire is also to start a family with her.

The ideal for a baby is a mother dedicated to this wonderful mission, at least the first years of her life that are so crucial in the life of children and if that protection and care could be extended to her teenage life it would be wonderful.

Nowadays, in these times when women already occupy jobs in society, it would be wise to consider that the profession of being a mother is one of the most beautiful and unforgettable; It is the best time spent in the life of every woman!

Fortunately, some women have chosen to Educate at Home, others can work online and take close care of their home and children.

A woman who has just given birth should have only one thought in her mind: to raise her child knowing that everything they need to live is provided by a responsible, loving and protective man.

CHAPTER XIII: EMOTIONS, SYMPTOMS AND SOLUTIONS

It is true that many times there are certain extreme emotions that do not belong to us and we live them as ours. They may have developed from a difficult labor situation, from the mother's own anxiety both during pregnancy and at the time of delivery. Even before getting pregnant. Remember, just as we inherit the physical DNA, we also inherit the emotional DNA.

During this life those limitations that we have, instead of accepting them as a fact, we must find the source of provenance. We can't change anything if you don't know where it comes from and what needs to be changed.

Let's talk roughly about some of these emotions.

DISTRESS AND LACK OF FAITH IN YOURSELF AND OTHERS.

This distrust can be towards oneself and / or others. This lack of faith hinders the progress towards the goals that each person has set in their life. It is like a large stone hanging from the neck and that does not allow steps to be taken safely. What could have happened? I will give some examples:

1. The mother got pregnant before getting married and that caused her to have to leave school.
2. The married mother expecting a baby suddenly found herself alone due to her husband's departure or death. When the unborn baby experiences a loss of the father, in this case lives with the mistaken belief that no one will be there to help him.

The mother's reaction to these two possible cases is very important, some women accept their pregnancy condition immediately, but in the vast majority it is not. There is surprise, frustration, loneliness, distrust, sadness, the feeling of rejection, abandonment. The situation is that nobody explains to the baby about what is happening, the whole focus is on the mother, who is a victim of the circumstances. She even forgets the importance of talking to the unborn baby in those delicate moments of painful emotions.

That baby will grow up with the idea that he is not welcome, and that being accepted is a challenge, he will think that to be loved and accepted by others he has often to 'beg' for love. The person will live trying to please others, in this way, it will be difficult for her or him to find a person with whom to share their life in a healthy and harmonious way.

All these negative emotions and thoughts affect the emotional and physical health of the human being. Then the disease appears, which is used as a way of life. It is the loss of harmony and balance between body and mind. Our body manifests the changes in consciousness that we have and then the symptoms of the disease appear. The disease as such has a purpose: to call our attention to the lack of care for ourselves and help us to make changes in that specific issue and make ourselves healthy.

I recommend reading the book 'Illness as a Way' (1983) by Dethlefsen , Thorwald / Dahlke, Ruediger . If you are interested in topics of psychology and healing.

In the year of 1995 I attended a very interesting Workshop called "Knowing Myself Through My Body" based on the principles of Wilhelm Reich (March 24, 1897 - November 3, 1957) doctor of medicine and psychology born in Austria, who had a radical opinion as for the expression of the individual's personality through body movements.

This photograph of the Personality Analysis of an adult client reveals his anguish and pain at birth, followed by the absence of a father and the extreme vulnerability of his mother, a very unfavorable environment to start his life cycle.

I present this beautiful CIP method© (Cognitive Image Profiling) also known as Cognitive Profile.

Here you can find the blockages and the potential that exist in an individual in order to heal stories, break patterns and transcend.

Each card has a symbolism, and this interpretation is unique for each individual because the client selects the cards in two different ways, the therapist just gives the interpretation depending on what the client has chosen, where it is placed, with which other card is flanked, in what position, etc.

There is great disappointment in this client, since she has loaded herself with responsibilities that do not belong to her, she becomes impatient, anxious and distrustful which leads her to a severe depression, her current purpose is to rebuild her life, leave the burden she has been imposed, she wants a new beginning and stability. She did not have a father present and her mother submitted without fighting for what she wanted, a single mother, she was an emotionally disabled woman and the daughter (my client) since an early age took the responsibility of taking care for her.

Thus, we also have people with great anger towards themselves without realizing that they are carrying the emotions of their ancestors, making them their own. In an analysis of Cognitive Imaging Profile, we can read an incredible story from the gestation of the individual and in that way help the person to find the solution of that unpleasant situation. This is the study of an 8-year-old girl with a history of rejection and verbal abuse by her biological father and the work with this child is supported by the mother or adoptive parents to help her assess her true self as a child and her talents.

Unfortunately, here there is a loss of illusion and if it not helped on time, then she could grow up with the belief that men reject her and they must be pleased no matter the consequences in order to 'win' their acceptance and their love. Not a good start in life. But everything can be changed with love